# my **revision** notes

# AS Edexcel History
# STALIN'S RUSSIA
# 1924–53

Robin Bunce and
Laura Gallagher

Faizah

**HODDER**
EDUCATION
AN HACHETTE UK COMPANY

**Cover photo** © Galina – Fotolia

Every effort has been made to trace all copyright holders, but if any have been inadvertently overlooked the Publishers will be pleased to make the necessary arrangements at the first opportunity.

Although every effort has been made to ensure that website addresses are correct at time of going to press, Hodder Education cannot be held responsible for the content of any website mentioned in this book. It is sometimes possible to find a relocated web page by typing in the address of the home page for a website in the URL window of your browser.

Hachette UK's policy is to use papers that are natural, renewable and recyclable products and made from wood grown in sustainable forests. The logging and manufacturing processes are expected to conform to the environmental regulations of the country of origin.

**Orders:** please contact Bookpoint Ltd, 130 Milton Park, Abingdon, Oxon OX14 4SB. Telephone: +44 (0)1235 827720. Fax: +44 (0)1235 400454. Lines are open 9.00a.m.–5.00p.m., Monday to Saturday, with a 24-hour message answering service. Visit our website at www.hoddereducation. co.uk.

© Robin Bunce and Laura Gallagher 2011
First published in 2011 by
Hodder Education,
an Hachette UK company
338 Euston Road
London NW1 3BH

Impression number     10  9  8  7  6  5  4  3  2  1
Year                      2015  2014  2013  2012  2011

All rights reserved. Apart from any use permitted under UK copyright law, no part of this publication may be reproduced or transmitted in any form or by any means, electronic or mechanical, including photocopying and recording, or held within any information storage and retrieval system, without permission in writing from the publisher or under licence from the Copyright Licensing Agency Limited. Further details of such licences (for reprographic reproduction) may be obtained from the Copyright Licensing Agency Limited, Saffron House, 6–10 Kirby Street, London EC1N 8TS.

Typeset in 11pt Stempel Schneidler by Pantek Media, Maidstone, Kent
Artwork by Pantek Media
Printed and bound in India

A catalogue record for this title is available from the British Library

ISBN 978 1 444 15207 4

# Contents

# Introduction

## About Unit 1

Unit 1 is worth 50 per cent of your AS level. It requires detailed knowledge of a historical period and the ability to explain the causes, consequences and significance of historical events. There are no sources in the Unit 1 exam and therefore all marks available are awarded for use of your own knowledge.

In the exam, you are required to answer two questions from a range of options. The exam lasts for one hour and twenty minutes, unless you have been awarded extra time. The questions are all worth 30 marks and therefore you should divide your time equally between the questions.

The questions you answer must be on different topics. This book deals exclusively with topic D4: Stalin's Russia 1924–53. However, you must also be prepared to answer a question on another topic.

The exam will test your ability to:

- select information that focuses on the question
- organise this information to provide an answer to the question
- show range and depth in the examples you provide
- analyse the significance of the information used to reach an overall judgement.

## Stalin's Russia 1924–53

The specification states that students should study four general areas as part of this topic.

1. The struggle for power 1924–29.
2. Transforming the Soviet Union – collectivisation and industrialisation.
3. Persecution and control – the totalitarian regime.
4. The making of a superpower – the impact of the Second World War.

## How to use this book

This book has been designed to help you to develop the knowledge and skills necessary to succeed in the exam. The book is divided into four sections – one for each general area of the course. Each section is made up of a series of topics organised into double-page spreads. On the left-hand page, you will find a summary of the key content you need to learn. Words in bold in the key content are defined in the glossary (see page 60). On the right-hand page, you will find exam-focused activities. Together, these two strands of the book will guide you through the knowledge and skills essential for exam success.

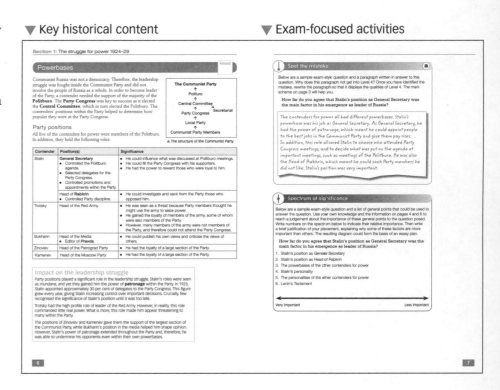

There are three levels of exam-focused activities.

- Band 1 activities are designed to develop the foundational skills needed to pass the exam. These have a blue heading and this symbol:
- Band 2 activities are designed to build on the skills developed in Band 1 activities and to help you achieve a C grade. These have an orange heading and this symbol:
- Band 3 activities are designed to enable you to access the highest grades. These have a purple heading and this symbol:

Some of the activities have answers or suggested answers on pages 64–68 and have the following symbol to indicate this: (a)

Others are intended for you to complete in pairs and assess by comparing answers. These do not have answers provided.

Each section ends with an exam-style question, and a model A-grade answer with examiner's commentary. This should give you guidance on what is required to achieve the top grades.

You can also keep track of your revision by ticking off each topic heading in the book, or by ticking the checklist on the contents page. Tick each box when you have:

- revised and understood a topic
- completed the activities.

## Mark scheme

For some of the activities in this book, it will be useful to refer to the mark scheme for the unit. Below is the mark scheme for Unit 1.

| Level | Marks | Description |
|---|---|---|
| 1 | 1–6 | <ul><li>Lacks focus on the question.</li><li>Limited factual accuracy.</li><li>Highly generalised.</li></ul>*Level 1 answers are highly simplistic, irrelevant or vague.* |
| 2 | 7–12 | <ul><li>General points with some focus on the question.</li><li>Some accurate and relevant supporting evidence.</li></ul>*Level 2 answers might tell the story without addressing the question, or address the question without providing supporting examples.* |
| 3 | 13–18 | <ul><li>General points that focus on the question.</li><li>Accurate support, but this may be either only partly relevant or lacking detail, or both.</li><li>Attempted analysis.</li></ul>*Level 3 answers attempt to focus on the question, but have significant areas of weakness. For example, the focus on the question may drift, the answer may lack specific examples, or parts of the essay may simply tell the story. Answers that do not deal with factors that are stated in the question cannot achieve higher than Level 3.* |
| 4 | 19–24 | <ul><li>General points that clearly focus on the question and show understanding of the most important factors involved.</li><li>Accurate, relevant and detailed supporting evidence.</li><li>Analysis.</li></ul>*Level 4 answers clearly attempt to answer the question and demonstrate a detailed and wide-ranging knowledge of the period studied.* |
| 5 | 25–30 | <ul><li>As Level 4</li><li>Sustained analysis.</li></ul>*Level 5 answers are thorough and detailed. They clearly engage with the question and offer a balanced and carefully reasoned argument, which is sustained throughout the essay.* |

# Section 1:
## The struggle for power 1924–29

Revised

## The contenders for power

### Background to the leadership struggle

In 1924, Lenin, the first leader of **communist** Russia, died. Lenin had led the **October Revolution** of 1917 and guided the new government through its first crucial years. Lenin left no clear indication of who should succeed him, and on his death, five leading **Bolsheviks** fought to replace him.

## Personalities

### Stalin

Members of the **Soviet** government called Stalin 'the grey blur', meaning that there was nothing outstanding or controversial about him. He had played a minor role in the October Revolution and in the **Russian Civil War**. However, his real gift was for administration, and due to his **peasant** upbringing he understood the way that many ordinary Russians thought and acted. He also had a reputation for loyalty to Lenin. Nonetheless, when Lenin became ill, Stalin started disobeying his orders. **Lenin's Testament** criticised him for this, but, as the *Testament* was kept secret, Lenin's final instruction that Stalin should be sacked from his position within the Party was not widely known.

### Trotsky

Trotsky was the most heroic of the contenders. Together with Lenin, he had planned and led the October Revolution and had commanded the **Red Army** during the Civil War. He was extremely glamorous, and a gifted **theorist** and orator, who inspired the loyalty of his troops. Trotsky had a radical vision for the future of Russia, which appealed to young and idealistic members of the Party. Indeed, Lenin's *Testament* praised Trotsky as 'the most outstanding member' of the Party. However, he was also viewed as arrogant and too western by many more cautious communists who were reluctant to trust him because he only joined the **Bolshevik Party** in 1917.

### Bukharin

Bukharin was the youngest of the contenders. Like Trotsky, he was known as a thinker and an orator. However, he lacked Trotsky's arrogance, and for this reason Lenin described him as the 'favourite' of the whole Party. Following the Civil War, he became the leading advocate of the **New Economic Policy (NEP)**, a compromise between communism and **capitalism**. Some older communists thought Bukharin was too young to lead the Party, and radicals on the **left wing** were suspicious of his economic policy. What is more, Lenin's *Testament* criticised Bukharin's theories as they were 'not fully **Marxist**'.

### Zinoviev and Kamenev

Zinoviev and Kamenev were Lenin's closest friends. Indeed, they were among the first members of the Bolshevik Party. However, in spite of this, they had a history of disloyalty and cowardice. They publically criticised Lenin's plans for the October Revolution. During the Civil War, Zinoviev avoided the fighting by staying in the most expensive hotel in **Petrograd**, surrounded by prostitutes.

## ! Complete the paragraph

Below are a sample exam-style question and a paragraph written in answer to this question. The paragraph contains a point and a concluding explanatory link back to the question, but lacks specific examples. Complete the paragraph adding examples in the space provided.

**How far were personal factors the main reason for Stalin's emergence as leader of Russia?**

> Personal factors were very important in Stalin's emergence as leader of Russia. For example
> 
> _____
> 
> _____
> 
> _____
> 
> _____
> 
> In this way, personal factors played an important role in Stalin's emergence as leader because Trotsky's arrogance, Bukharin's youth, and Zinoviev and Kamenev's cowardice made these contenders unpopular with the Communist Party. However, Stalin had no obvious flaws.

## ⧫ Identify an argument

Below are a series of definitions, a sample exam-style question and two sample conclusions. One of the conclusions achieves a high level because it contains an argument. The other achieves a lower level because it contains only description and assertion. Identify which is which. The mark scheme on page 3 will help you.

- **Description:** a detailed account.
- **Assertion:** a statement of fact or an opinion that is not supported by a reason.
- **Reason:** a statement that explains or justifies something.
- **Argument:** an assertion justified with a reason.

**How far were personal factors the main reason for Stalin's emergence as leader of Russia?**

> Overall, personal factors played a key role in Stalin's emergence as leader of Russia. This is because Stalin's personality was ideally suited to manipulating the Party that had emerged after Lenin's death. Stalin was the best administrator; he understood the desires of peasants and therefore he was able to influence the Party in ways that the other contenders did not understand. Consequently, while other factors, such as ideology and the economy, played important roles, Stalin's personality was the most important because it gave him an advantage over the other contenders.

> In conclusion, personal factors played a large role in Stalin's emergence as Russia's leader. Stalin was described as 'the grey blur' meaning he had a job that other contenders thought was boring. Trotsky was arrogant, Bukharin was a young intellectual, and Zinoviev and Kamenev had been Lenin's best friends, but in the end, it was Stalin who emerged as leader, and his personality played a big role.

## Powerbases

Revised

Communist Russia was not a democracy. Therefore, the leadership struggle was fought inside the Communist Party and did not involve the people of Russia as a whole. In order to become leader of the Party, a contender needed the support of the majority of the **Politburo**. The **Party Congress** was key to success as it elected the **Central Committee**, which in turn elected the Politburo. The contenders' positions within the Party helped to determine how popular they were at the Party Congress.

**The Communist Party**
↑
Polituro
↑
Central Committee ↘
↑            Secretariat
Party Congress
↑
Local Party
↑
Communist Party Members

▲ The structure of the Communist Party.

### Party positions

All five of the contenders for power were members of the Politburo. In addition, they held the following roles:

| Contender | Position(s) | Significance |
|---|---|---|
| Stalin | **General Secretary**<br>• Controlled the Politburo agenda.<br>• Selected delegates for the Party Congress.<br>• Controlled promotions and appointments within the Party. | • He could influence what was discussed at Politburo meetings.<br>• He could fill the Party Congress with his supporters.<br>• He had the power to reward those who were loyal to him. |
|  | Head of **Rabkrin**<br>• Controlled Party discipline. | • He could investigate and sack from the Party those who opposed him. |
| Trotsky | Head of the Red Army. | • He was seen as a threat because Party members thought he might use the army to seize power.<br>• He gained the loyalty of members of the army, some of whom were also members of the Party.<br>• However, many members of the army were not members of the Party, and therefore could not attend the Party Congress. |
| Bukharin | Head of the Media<br>• Editor of **Pravda**. | • He could publish his own views and criticise the views of others. |
| Zinoviev | Head of the Petrograd Party | • He had the loyalty of a large section of the Party. |
| Kamenev | Head of the Moscow Party | • He had the loyalty of a large section of the Party. |

### Impact on the leadership struggle

Party positions played a significant role in the leadership struggle. Stalin's roles were seen as mundane, and yet they gained him the power of **patronage** within the Party. In 1923, Stalin appointed approximately 30 per cent of delegates to the Party Congress. This figure grew every year, giving Stalin increasing control over important decisions. Crucially, few recognised the significance of Stalin's position until it was too late.

Trotsky had the high profile role of leader of the Red Army. However, in reality, this role commanded little real power. What is more, this role made him appear threatening to many within the Party.

The positions of Zinoviev and Kamenev gave them the support of the largest section of the Communist Party, while Bukharin's position in the media helped him shape opinion. However, Stalin's power of patronage extended throughout the Party and, therefore, he was able to undermine his opponents even within their own powerbases.

## Spot the mistake

Below are a sample exam-style question and a paragraph written in answer to this question. Why does this paragraph not get into Level 4? Once you have identified the mistake, rewrite the paragraph so that it displays the qualities of Level 4. The mark scheme on page 3 will help you.

How far do you agree that Stalin's position as General Secretary was the main factor in his emergence as leader of Russia?

The contenders for power all had different powerbases. Stalin's powerbase was his job as General Secretary. As General Secretary, he had the power of patronage, which meant he could appoint people to the best jobs in the Communist Party and give them pay rises. In addition, this role allowed Stalin to choose who attended Party Congress meetings, and to decide what was put on the agenda at important meetings, such as meetings of the Politburo. He was also the Head of Rabkrin, which meant he could sack Party members he did not like. Stalin's position was very important.

## Spectrum of significance

Below are a sample exam-style question and a list of general points that could be used to answer the question. Use your own knowledge and the information on pages 4 and 6 to reach a judgement about the importance of these general points to the question posed. Write numbers on the spectrum below to indicate their relative importance. Then write a brief justification of your placement, explaining why some of these factors are more important than others. The resulting diagram could form the basis of an essay plan.

How far do you agree that Stalin's position as General Secretary was the main factor in his emergence as leader of Russia?

1. Stalin's position as General Secretary
2. Stalin's position as Head of Rabkrin
3. The powerbases of the other contenders for power
4. Stalin's personality
5. The personalities of the other contenders for power
6. Lenin's *Testament*

← ─────────────────────────────── →

Very important                                    Less important

## Ideology: the great industrialisation debate

### Economic and ideological problems

Communists had always anticipated that the first successful revolution would take place in an advanced industrial economy. However, the Russian economy was primarily agricultural. This created a problem: how should the communists industrialise? There were two main schools of thought that divided the Party.

| Left-wing view: the dictatorship of industry | Right-wing view: the NEP |
|---|---|
| • High taxes for the peasants in order to fund industrialisation.<br>• Encourage the peasants to join **collective farms** to increase agricultural productivity.<br>• Rapid state-funded industrialisation. | • Low taxes for the peasants in order to fund gradual industrialisation.<br>• Allow peasants to own their own farms and trade on the **free market** to ensure the popularity of the regime.<br>• Slow state-funded industrialisation. |

Trotsky argued passionately for the left-wing solution of rapid industrialisation. He believed that the dictatorship of industry was a fully communist policy, unlike the semi-capitalist NEP. Bukharin was the leading advocate of the right-wing solution, initially with the support of Stalin, Zinoviev and Kamenev.

### The rise and fall of the NEP

The NEP was extremely popular in the Communist Party in the early 1920s. Many communists were unwilling to increase taxation on the peasants because they feared a backlash against the government. Moreover, the NEP was creating economic growth and increasing the production of consumer goods. However, in 1927 growth figures were much lower than expected. As a result, support for the NEP decreased.

|  | 1925 | 1926 | 1927 | 1928 |
|---|---|---|---|---|
| Grain (million tonnes) | 73 | 77 | 72 | 73 |

▲ Grain production during the NEP. An increase in grain production meant a better standard of living for the Russian people.

### Impact on the leadership struggle

The initial success of the NEP ensured the popularity of the **right wing**. Between 1924 and 1925, all of the contenders except Trotsky backed the NEP. Trotsky's arguments in favour of rapid industrialisation looked foolhardy: the NEP was helping the Russian economy to grow and Trotsky's alternative was untested. This undermined Trotsky's bid to become leader of Russia.

In 1925, Zinoviev and Kamenev abandoned the NEP in an attempt to win the support of the left wing of the Party. However, the continuing success of the NEP meant that this attempt to gain control of the Party was doomed to failure.

Stalin only abandoned the NEP in 1928, once it was clearly failing and the Party was more sympathetic to more radical left-wing economic solutions. In this way, his move from the right wing to the left wing increased his popularity. By contrast, Bukharin continued to argue for the NEP and lost credibility as a result.

## Eliminate irrelevance

**(a)**

Below are a sample exam-style question and a paragraph written in answer to this question. Read the paragraph and identify parts that are not directly relevant to the question. Draw a line through the information that is irrelevant and justify your deletions in the margin.

**Why had Stalin emerged as leader of Russia by 1928?**

One reason why Stalin emerged as leader of Russia was due to the debate about the economy within the Communist Party. The Party was divided between the left wing, which favoured rapid industrialisation, and the right wing, which wanted to continue with the NEP. The NEP favoured the peasants as it allowed them to trade freely and make a profit. Stalin was born into a peasant family in Georgia. The right wing argued that this was necessary as peasants formed the majority of the population and their loyalty was important for the survival of the government. The left wing criticised the NEP because it wasn't fully communist. Communism was an idea developed by Karl Marx, a famous German philosopher in the nineteenth century. He thought that history went through different economic stages. The left wing argued that rapid industrialisation was necessary if communism was to survive. The economic debate was very important to Stalin's emergence as leader of Russia because he was able to use the debate first against the left wing, and then, once the NEP started to fail, against the right wing. In this way, he knocked out his opponents.

## Develop the detail

**(a)**

Below are a sample exam-style question and a paragraph written in answer to this question. The paragraph contains a limited amount of detail. Annotate the paragraph to add additional detail to the answer.

**How far do you agree that economic debates within the Communist Party were the main reason why Stalin emerged as leader of Russia?**

Economic debates played a major role in Stalin's emergence as leader of Russia. The Party was divided over this issue. Some communists wanted to continue with the NEP as they felt this would make the Communist Party more popular in Russia. Others wanted rapid industrialisation for ideological reasons. In the late 1920s, the NEP began to fail badly and this had an impact on the debate. For example, Stalin switched sides in order to win more support. Previously, Zinoviev and Kamenev had also switched sides, but this had not benefited them. In this way, economic debates decreased support for all contenders for power, except Stalin. Only Stalin used the debates to his advantage.

## Ideology: foreign policy

Revised

### Russia and the world

In 1917, Lenin and the Bolsheviks believed that the revolution in Russia would spark revolutions across the world. They assumed that Russia would be one communist country among many. However, by 1921, it was obvious that world revolution was some way off. Leading communists responded to this unexpected situation in two main ways.

| Left-wing view: permanent revolution | Right-wing view: Socialism in One Country |
| --- | --- |
| <ul><li>No **socialist** society can exist on its own.</li><li>Communist Russia will only be secure once successful revolutions have occurred in other countries.</li><li>Aggressive foreign policy.</li></ul> | <ul><li>**Socialism** can be built in Russia alone.</li><li>Russia will lead the rest of the world to communism in time.</li><li>There is no immediate need to incite revolutions in other countries.</li></ul> |

Divisions over Russia's role in the world emerged in 1924. Bukharin and Stalin advocated Socialism in One Country. By contrast, Trotsky argued for permanent revolution. In 1925, after their break with the right wing of the Party, Zinoviev and Kamenev also backed the idea of permanent revolution.

### Impact on the leadership struggle

The debate over Russian foreign policy was crucial to the outcome of the leadership struggle. Socialism in One Country had much greater appeal to communists for three reasons.

- Socialism in One Country appealed to Russian **nationalism** because it stressed Russia's importance as the first communist country.

- Permanent revolution appeared defeatist as many communists felt that this suggested communism in Russia was doomed because the revolution in Europe had not occurred.

- Permanent revolution was seen as much more dangerous because many people feared it would lead to war. For Russians who had lived through the First World War and the Civil War, this was a daunting prospect.

In this way, the debate over foreign policy placed the left wing of the Party at a disadvantage. Stalin and Bukharin were able to use the debate to discredit first Trotsky and then, after 1925, Zinoviev and Kamenev.

## ! Delete as applicable

Below are a sample exam-style question and a paragraph written in answer to this question. Read the paragraph and decide which option (in bold) is most appropriate. Delete the least appropriate options and complete the paragraph by justifying your selection.

**How far do you agree that ideological debates about economics and foreign policy were the main reason why Stalin emerged as leader of Russia?**

Ideological debates played a **great role/some role/a limited role** in Stalin's emergence as leader of Russia. The left wing's economic policy was appealing because rapid industrialisation was bold and fully communist. However, left-wing views on foreign policy allowed Stalin to accuse Trotsky of being too aggressive in his desire to promote revolution across the world. Equally, the right wing's vision of Socialism in One Country appealed to the many nationalists in the Communist Party. However, the NEP, even when successful, remained a capitalist compromise, which many in the Party found uninspiring. In this way, ideological debates were **extremely/moderately/slightly** significant in Stalin's emergence as leader of Russia because

_____

_____

## ! Turning assertion into argument

Below are a sample exam-style question and a series of assertions. Read the question and then add a justification to each of the assertions to turn it into an argument.

**How far was the debate over foreign policy within the Communist Party responsible for Stalin's emergence as leader of Soviet Russia?**

The debate over Trotsky's idea of permanent revolution was crucial to the outcome of the leadership struggle because

_____

_____

Stalin's arguments for Socialism in One Country played an important role in helping him become leader of Russia because

_____

_____

The debate over economic policy was more important in deciding the outcome of the leadership struggle than the debate over foreign policy because

_____

_____

## Making and breaking alliances

### Power vacuum

Lenin's death created a power vacuum at the heart of Soviet government. Between 1923 and 1928 Russian politics was dominated by a series of **factions** and alliances, as the table shows. Alliances that commanded a majority of support in the Politburo formed the government. Minority alliances formed the opposition.

### Triumvirate versus Left Opposition

The Triumvirate was formed in order to prevent Trotsky seizing power. Trotsky was the best known of the contenders for power and his ambition to become Russia's next ruler was widely known. In 1924, at the Thirteenth Party Congress, the Triumvirate successfully defended the NEP against Trotsky's left-wing alternative. Trotsky's failure to win the vote at the Congress appeared to be the end of his leadership ambitions.

### Duumvirate versus United Opposition

Having defeated Trotsky, the Triumvirate had lost its common enemy and consequently, the alliance fell apart. Zinoviev and Kamenev moved to the left wing of the Party and advocated rapid industrialisation. Stalin allied with Bukharin to defend the NEP and Socialism in One Country, an alliance known as the Duumvirate. In 1927, the Fifteenth Party Congress voted against the United Opposition (which now included Trotsky) and in favour of the Duumvirate's policies.

|  | Government | Opposition |
|---|---|---|
| **1923–25** | Triumvirate <br> • Zinoviev <br> • Kamenev <br> • Stalin | Left Opposition <br> • Trotsky |
| **1925–28** | Duumvirate <br> • Bukharin <br> • Stalin | United Opposition <br> • Trotsky <br> • Zinoviev <br> • Kamenev |
| **1928–29** | Stalin | Right Opposition <br> • Bukharin |

▲ Alliances during the power struggle.

### Stalin versus Right Opposition

Following their defeat, Trotsky, Zinoviev and Kamenev were expelled from the Communist Party. At the same time, the NEP was clearly failing. Stalin abandoned the NEP and adopted left-wing economic policies. In so doing, he won the support of the left wing of the Party. Bukharin remained committed to the NEP, and as it failed, his credibility within the Party diminished.

### Stalin victorious

In 1928, Stalin introduced emergency economic measures, which effectively ended the NEP. Bukharin challenged this, but at a meeting of the Central Committee senior communists voted in favour of Stalin's measures. Stalin's victory before the Central Committee confirmed that he alone was the ruler of Soviet Russia.

### Impact on the leadership struggle

Alliances played an extremely important role in the leadership struggle. First, the alliances allowed Stalin to stay in the background while the other contenders fought each other in public. In 1924, it was Zinoviev and Kamenev who publically did battle with Trotsky, while in 1927, it was Bukharin who spoke out against the United Opposition. In this way, Stalin distanced himself from petty squabbling and gained the respect of the Party. Secondly, the alliances allowed Stalin to deal with his opponents in turn: in 1924, the Triumvirate was able to defeat Trotsky; in 1927, the Duumvirate dealt with Zinoviev and Kamenev. Finally, Stalin's alliances allowed him to maintain a majority of support in the Politburo. In this way, Stalin was always part of the government and never associated with an opposition faction.

## Simple essay style

Below is a sample exam-style question. Use your own knowledge and the information on the opposite page to produce a plan for an answer to this question. Choose four general points, and provide three pieces of specific information to support each point. Once you have planned your essay, write the introduction and conclusion for the essay. The introduction should list the points to be discussed in the essay. The conclusion should summarise the key points and justify which point was the most important.

**How far do you agree that Stalin's ability to make and break alliances was the main reason for his emergence as leader of Russia by 1928?**

## You're the examiner

Below are a sample exam-style question and a paragraph written in answer to this question. Read the paragraph and the mark scheme provided on page 3. Decide which level you would award the paragraph. Write the level below, along with a justification for your decision.

**Why had Stalin emerged as leader of Soviet Russia by 1928?**

One reason why Stalin emerged as leader of Soviet Russia was his ability to make and break alliances. First, alliances allowed Stalin to remove his opponents in turn. For example, by 1924 Stalin, united with Zinoviev and Kamenev in the Triumvirate, had defeated Trotsky in the debate over the future of the NEP. In addition, Stalin, united with Bukharin in the Duumvirate, defeated Trotsky, Zinoviev and Kamenev at the Fifteenth Party Congress in 1927. Secondly, Stalin was able to use his alliances with other members of the Communist Party to remain distanced from the squabbling over ideology that characterised much of the power struggle. At the Thirteenth Party Congress in 1924, Zinoviev and Kamenev criticised Trotsky's policy of rapid industrialisation and in 1927 Bukharin criticised the United Opposition for the same reasons. Thirdly, Stalin was able to use alliances to ensure that he remained in the government. In this way, Stalin's ability to make and break alliances helped him to become leader of Soviet Russia because he maintained his own influence and popularity in the Communist Party at the same time as denying his opponents' power.

Level:    Reasons for choosing this level:

13

## Devious tactics

### Dirty tricks

In addition to his powerbase and his use of alliances, Stalin was also willing to use dirty tricks to gain power.

### Lenin's funeral

Lenin's funeral in 1924 was highly significant because it gave the contenders for power a platform from which to show their loyalty to Lenin. Stalin used Lenin's funeral to discredit Trotsky. Trotsky was convalescing on the shores of the Black Sea at the time that Lenin died and therefore was cut off from events in Moscow. Stalin used this to his advantage by telling Trotsky the wrong date for the funeral. As a result, Trotsky missed the funeral and was regarded as disloyal to Lenin.

### Lenin's *Testament*

Lenin's *Testament* had instructed senior communists to remove Stalin from his position. Stalin persuaded Zinoviev and Kamenev, who were also criticised in the *Testament*, to argue that Stalin should remain in post and that the *Testament* should not be published. Their arguments convinced the Central Committee and therefore the vast majority of the Communist Party never learnt of Lenin's judgement.

### Bukharin's medical

Following Stalin's split with Bukharin in 1928, Stalin used his influence as General Secretary to prevent Bukharin from attending important meetings. On one occasion, Bukharin was travelling by air to reach a meeting of the Central Committee. Stalin arranged to have Bukharin's plane grounded twice, insisting that Bukharin undergo a series of medical checks. As a result, Bukharin missed an opportunity to extend his influence within the Central Committee.

### Faction fighting

In 1921, Lenin had banned factions from the Communist Party. In 1928, Stalin circulated rumours that he was about to form an alliance with Zinoviev and Kamenev. In order to prevent this, Bukharin called a secret meeting with Zinoviev and Kamenev. Stalin had anticipated this, and had placed Bukharin under surveillance. Stalin revealed the secret meeting to the Central Committee, accusing Bukharin of **factionalism**.

### Ideological tactics

Stalin's move from the right wing to the left wing in 1928 was extremely significant. By adopting rapid industrialisation as his economic policy, and maintaining Socialism in One Country as his foreign policy, Stalin united the most popular policies in the Party at the time. Rapid industrialisation was seen as heroic and had grown in popularity as the NEP began to fail. Socialism in One Country remained popular as it appealed to Russian nationalism. Moreover, by uniting policies from the left wing and the right wing, Stalin was able to win support from both sides of the Party (see table).

| | Left wing | Stalin | Right wing |
|---|---|---|---|
| **Economic policy** | Rapid industrialisation ☺ ➞ | ☺ | NEP ☹ |
| **Foreign policy** | Permanent revolution ☹ | ☺ ⟵ | Socialism in One Country ☺ |

▲ Support for Stalin.

### Impact on the leadership struggle

Stalin's dirty tricks gave him an important advantage at crucial moments of the leadership struggle, and enabled him to discredit his main rivals for power. Stalin's ideological shift in 1928 allowed him to present the most appealing mix of policies to the Party, to retain a large measure of support from the right wing, while, at the same time, attracting new support from the left wing.

## Support or challenge?

Below is a sample exam-style question, which asks how far you agree with a specific statement. Below this is a series of general statements that are relevant to the question. Using your own knowledge and the information on the previous pages, decide whether these statements support or challenge the statement in the question and tick the appropriate box.

'It was Stalin's strengths rather than the weaknesses of his opponents that explain his rise to power.' How far do you agree with this statement?

|  | SUPPORT | CHALLENGE |
|---|---|---|
| Zinoviev and Kamenev agreed to help keep Lenin's *Testament* secret. |  |  |
| Trotsky missed Lenin's funeral. |  |  |
| Stalin was General Secretary of the Communist Party. |  |  |
| Stalin was known as 'the grey blur'. |  |  |
| Stalin was always in the governing alliance of the Communist Party. |  |  |
| Trotsky was perceived as being arrogant. |  |  |
| Bukharin remained committed to the NEP even when it failed. |  |  |

## RAG – Rate the timeline

Below are a sample exam-style question and a timeline. Read the question, study the timeline and, using three coloured pens, put a red, amber or green star next to the events to show:

- red – events and policies that have no relevance to the question
- amber – events and policies that have some significance to the question
- green – events and policies that are directly relevant to the question.

1. **Why was there a power struggle in Russia between 1924 and 1928?**

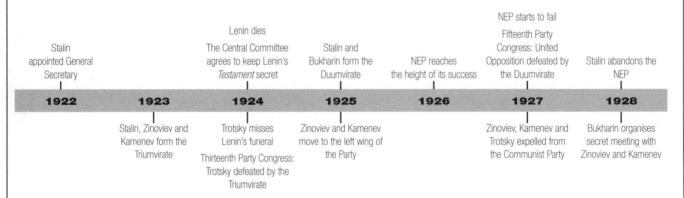

Now repeat the activity with the following questions. You could use different colours, or number your stars 1, 2 and 3.

2. **How far was the NEP the focus of the power struggle in Russia between 1924 and 1928?**

3. **Why did Stalin reject the NEP in 1928?**

## Recommended reading

Below is a list of suggested further reading on this topic.

- David Evans and Jane Jenkins, *Years of Russia and the USSR 1851–1991* (pages 265–270). Hodder and Stoughton, 2002.
- Dmitri Volkogonov, *The Rise and Fall of the Soviet Empire* (pages 83–103). Harper Collins, 1998.

## Exam focus

Below is a sample A-grade essay. Read the essay and the examiner's comments around it.

**How significant were ideological disputes in accounting for Stalin's emergence as leader of Russia?**

The introduction clearly answers the question and evaluates the relative importance of a series of factors, arguing that ideology was the most important factor in Stalin's rise to power. As a result, the introduction opens up the possibility of a mark within Level 5.

Ideological disputes were extremely significant in accounting for Stalin's emergence as leader of Russia. Disputes over the future of the economy and the future of foreign policy allowed the contenders for power to compete for support within the Communist Party by appealing to the different wings of the Party. Stalin's personality was also important in this process because he knew how to manipulate the debates to his advantage. His powerbase was also significant because it gave him a position from which he could exploit the divisions that the ideological battles had caused. Finally, Stalin's tactics allowed him to make the most of the advantages that came his way. Overall, the ideological disputes were the most significant factor as they allowed the contenders to fight publically and gain support within the Party.

This is a good opening sentence as it makes a clear point that is focused on the question.

Stalin used ideological disputes about the economy to seize power. On the left wing of the Party, Trotsky argued for a fully socialist policy. He wanted to abandon the NEP, which everyone acknowledged was a compromise with capitalism, and impose a 'dictatorship of industry'. In practice, this would mean imposing high taxes on the peasants to fund rapid industrialisation. Bukharin and the right wing disagreed, arguing that the NEP was successful as it allowed the economy to grow and was the best policy for a country in which peasants were the majority as it allowed peasants to make money on the free market.

The use of terms such as 'capitalism' and 'dictatorship of industry' demonstrate a good command of technical vocabulary.

Stalin used this debate to win power at the 1924 Party Congress. Siding with Zinoviev and Kamenev, the Triumvirate won the vote to continue the NEP and in so doing effectively eliminated Trotsky from the race. Similarly, in 1928, Stalin used economic disputes to gain power because, by moving from the right wing to the left wing, he isolated Bukharin at the very time the NEP was failing.

This paragraph concludes with a focused explanation, showing how the examples mentioned in the paragraph provide an answer to the question.

Stalin also used disputes about foreign policy to help him win power. Once again the Party was divided between the left wing and the right wing. Trotsky, Zinoviev and Kamenev criticised the right-wing view of Socialism in One Country. According to the left wing, it would be impossible to build Socialism in One Country because socialism required a world revolution. Bukharin and Stalin, on the other hand, argued that the left-wing's idea was dangerous because it implied imminent war between communist Russia and the rest of the world. Stalin used Socialism in One Country to win support within the Party because it appealed to Russian nationalism. In this way, Stalin became popular because nationalism was an important force in the Communist Party.

Stalin's personality was another key factor in his victory. Stalin was known as 'the grey blur'. By this, his colleagues meant that he was a man of moderation, unlike the colourful characters of Trotsky and Bukharin who took extreme positions within the Party. As the dispute between the left wing and the right wing raged, Stalin took a back seat, allowing his allies to argue in public. This helped Stalin gain power because he, unlike his opponents, looked like a moderate. This was very appealing to a party that was growing increasingly divided by ideological disputes.

> A clear explanation that shows the significance of Stalin's personality in the context of the ideological disputes.

Stalin's position within the Communist Party helped him to make the most of the ideological disputes. As the disputes raged between the left wing and the right wing, Stalin was able to win support through his power of patronage. Stalin was General Secretary of the Communist Party, which allowed him to promote people to important posts in the Party. As a result, he was able to count on the loyalty of an increasing number of Party members. Stalin's position in the Party helped him to win power because at meetings of the Party Congress and the Central Committee, Stalin could count on the support of an increasing number who owed their jobs to him.

Stalin was also an excellent tactician and this helped him to win power. Bukharin and Trotsky were far more intellectual than Stalin. Therefore, they always had the advantage when debating ideology. Stalin, however, was able to tactically exclude them from important meetings. In 1924, Stalin sent Trotsky the wrong date for Lenin's funeral and in 1928, Stalin arranged to have Bukharin's plane delayed so that he missed a crucial meeting of the Central Committee. In this way, Stalin's tactical excellence allowed him to win power because he was able to prevent his opponents challenging him at important meetings.

> Good use of dates and specific examples.

In conclusion, ideological disputes were the most important factor in determining who won the leadership of Russia. Disputes between the left wing and the right wing allowed the various contenders to win support from the different wings of the Party. Nonetheless, they were not the only factor. Stalin's personality, his position in the Party and his tactics enabled him to benefit from these disputes. Therefore, ideological debates were the most important factor because they initiated the public disputes which Stalin was able to turn to his advantage and win power.

> An excellent conclusion that ties together the whole essay, showing the way in which the different factors discussed come together to provide a sophisticated answer to the question.

**30/30**

This essay provides a detailed, focused and wide-ranging answer to the question. The sustained analysis, which starts in the introduction and is present in almost every paragraph from then on, allows the essay to enter Level 5. The detailed discussion of the stated factor and the fact that the essay deals with events from 1924 to 1928, and in so doing covers the entire period of the struggle, means that the essay gets a mark in the top band of the level.

## Reverse engineering

The best essays are based on careful plans. Read the essay and the examiner's comments and try to work out the general points of the plan used to write the essay. Once you have done this, note down the specific examples used to support each general point.

# Section 2:
## Transforming the Soviet Union – collectivisation and industrialisation

## Causes of modernisation

In 1928, Stalin launched his 'revolution from above', a revolution which would transform Russia's agriculture and industry. This economic modernisation came about for the following reasons.

### Economic reasons

Stalin had important economic reasons for transforming industry and agriculture. Since 1927, the NEP had failed to deliver increased economic growth in any sector of the economy, relative to 1926. In agriculture, the production of grain and livestock began to fall after 1926, leading to the **Grain Procurement Crisis**. In industry, output plateaued. Indeed, production under the NEP never exceeded pre-1914 levels. Stalin argued that the **free market**, which had characterised the NEP, needed to be replaced by economic planning in order to increase economic growth.

Industrialisation was a key goal of the communist government. Agricultural reform was essential for rapid industrialisation. Stalin planned to reorganise agriculture so that it was more efficient. This would provide the additional food needed for a growing industrial workforce, and release **peasants** to work in industry.

|  | 1913 | 1928 |
|---|---|---|
| Steel (millions of tonnes) | 4.0 | 4.0 |
| Iron (millions of tonnes) | 4.2 | 3.3 |

▲ Steel and iron production in Russia 1913–1928.

### Ideological reasons

The **communists** had always been critical of the free market. Indeed, even while the NEP was successful there was a significant section of the Party that favoured replacing **capitalism** with a more **socialist** system. Stalin's reforms in agriculture and industry replaced the free market with central planning, and therefore reflected the Party's long-standing ideological goals.

Many communists were concerned that the peasants preferred capitalism to communism. Stalin hoped that reforming agriculture would convince the peasants of the benefits of communism. In addition, Stalin believed that the NEP had favoured the peasants over the **working class**. As a communist, Stalin was committed to the welfare of the workers and therefore his economic reforms were designed to improve their living and working conditions.

### Political reasons

Stalin was keen to demonstrate that he had won the leadership struggle. By destroying the NEP, Stalin forced the **Central Committee** to choose between his policies and those of Bukharin. In choosing his policies, the Central Committee implicitly confirmed Stalin as leader of Russia.

### Fear of war

At the end of the 1920s, Russian officials feared that Germany was preparing for war. German industrial production far exceeded that of Russia, and in this sense, Germany was in a stronger position. In order to fight, Russia needed the modern industry necessary for rearmament.

## Complete the paragraph

**a**

Below are a sample exam-style question and a paragraph written in answer to this question. The paragraph contains a point and specific examples, but lacks a concluding explanatory link back to the question. Complete the paragraph by adding an explanatory link in the space provided.

**Why did Stalin launch his 'revolution from above' in economic policy in 1928?**

One reason why Stalin launched his 'revolution from above' in 1928 was that the NEP had failed. By 1928, the NEP had allowed steel production to recover to 1913 levels, that is to say 4 million tonnes were produced. However, iron production under the NEP was still considerably less than it had been before the First World War: iron production in 1913 had been 4.2 million tonnes, whereas in 1928 it was only 3.3 million tonnes. What is more, grain production under the NEP fell in 1927 and only partially recovered in 1928.

_____

_____

_____

## Spectrum of significance

Below are a sample exam-style question and a list of general points that could be used to answer the question. Use your own knowledge and the information on the opposite page to reach a judgement about the importance of these general points to the question posed. Write numbers on the spectrum below to indicate their relative importance. Then write a brief justification of your placement, explaining why some of these factors are more important than others. The resulting diagram could form the basis of an essay plan.

**Why did Stalin launch his 'revolution from above' in economic policy in 1928?**

1. The failure of the NEP
2. Plans to industrialise Russia
3. Desire to abolish the free market
4. The interests of the working class
5. The need to convince peasants of the benefits of communism
6. Stalin's desire to humiliate Bukharin
7. Fear of war

Very important ← ──────────────────────────── → Less important

## Collectivisation and its consequences

**Collectivisation** entailed merging small farms into large, mechanised farms where work and resources could be shared, leading to greater efficiency. Collectivisation was an attempt to solve the Grain Procurement Crisis, and therefore it went hand in hand with the persecution of **kulaks**, who Stalin suspected of hoarding grain.

## The stages of collectivisation

| Date | Event | Details |
|---|---|---|
| 1928 | Emergency measures | • Rationing introduced in cities, **requisitioning** introduced. |
| 1929 | Dekulakisation | • Compulsory collectivisation introduced.<br>• Kulaks rounded up and exiled by the **Red Army** and the secret police. |
| 1929 | Twenty-Five Thousanders | • 27,000 volunteers sent to the countryside to assist in dekulakisation. |
| 1930 | 'Dizzy with Success' | • Stalin halted compulsory collectivisation, blaming the chaos in the countryside on Party members being 'dizzy with success'.<br>• Farmers returned to their own farms. |
| 1931 | Collectivisation restarts | • Forced collectivisation began again, at a slower pace. |
| 1941 | Collectivisation complete | • All farms in Russia were collectivised. |

## The consequences of collectivisation

Despite Stalin's hopes, collectivisation was a disaster.

### Famine

Four factors led to the outbreak of famine in 1932.

■ Dekulakisation removed the most successful peasants from farms.

■ Forced collectivisation also led to the destruction of grain and livestock. Between 1929 and 1933, 18 million horses and 10 million sheep and goats were destroyed by peasants in protest at collectivisation.

■ The government set unrealistic targets for the new **collective farms**. Farms that failed to meet their target had all of their grain confiscated.

■ Although less grain was produced, more was exported to raise money for industrialisation: exports rose from 0.03 million tonnes in 1928 to 5 million tonnes in 1931.

Between 1932 and 1934, these four factors led to a widespread famine and the deaths of more than 10 million people. The Ukraine was especially hard hit as Stalin refused to allow any grain into the region to alleviate the famine.

### Effects on rural areas

■ Dekulakisation led to the exile of 10 million peasants. In some areas, as many as 10 per cent of peasants in a single village were exiled.

■ The harvest of 1933 was 10 million tonnes less than that of 1926.

■ By 1932, **machine tractor stations** had supplied 75,000 tractors to collective farms, which made up for the decline in the number of horses.

### Effects on urban areas

■ The standard of living of the working class fell sharply: bread was rationed, and by 1932 the amount of protein consumed by workers had fallen by 66 per cent.

■ Famine in the countryside led to increasing urbanisation: the population of some cities trebled between 1930 and 1940.

## Spot the mistake

**(a)**

Below are a sample exam-style question and a paragraph written in answer to this question. Why does this paragraph not get into Level 4? Once you have identified the mistake, rewrite the paragraph so that it displays the qualities of Level 4. The mark scheme on page 3 will help you.

**How far do you agree that collectivisation was a failure?**

> Collectivisation began in 1929. Stalin's first attempt to collectivise was met with stiff resistance and, as a result, he sent out the Red Army and the secret police to arrest kulaks, that is to say, rich peasants. Stalin continued this overall policy in 1929, when he sent 27,000 volunteers, known as the Twenty-Five Thousanders, to supervise collectivisation. However, in reality the Twenty-Five Thousanders were actually used to assist in dekulakisation rather than collectivisation. The next year, Stalin stopped both dekulakisation and collectivisation because Party members were 'dizzy with success'. But collectivisation began again in 1931, although at a much slower pace. By 1941, it was clear that collectivisation had been a complete success because 100 per cent of farms in Russia were collectivised.

## Simple essay style

Below are three sample exam-style questions. Use your own knowledge and the information on the opposite page to produce plans for these questions. For each plan, choose four general points, and provide three pieces of specific information to support each general point. Once you have planned each essay, write the introduction and conclusion for the essay. The introduction should list the points to be discussed in the essay. The conclusion should summarise the key points and justify which point was the most important.

**How far do you agree that the peasantry were the main victims of collectivisation?**

**How accurate is it to say that collectivisation was a disaster for the Russian people in the years 1928–1941?**

**Why did collectivisation have such disastrous consequences for Russia's peasantry?**

## The First Five-Year Plan 1928–32

Revised

Stalin admitted that Russian industry was a hundred years behind the west. He aimed to use Five-Year Plans to ensure that Russia caught up within fifteen years.

### The nature of the First Five-Year Plan

The planned economy was administered by **Gosplan**, which set targets for production across Russia. The Plan focused on heavy industry – coal, oil, iron and steel – for two reasons.

- These industries produced the raw materials needed for future economic development and for rearmament.
- The majority of Russian workers, many of whom had been peasants, had little experience of industry and therefore were better suited to the relatively uncomplicated tasks involved in heavy industry.

### Successes of the First Five-Year Plan

#### Production

Russia's economy grew at a phenomenal 14 per cent per year during the First Five-Year Plan. Output exceeded production under the NEP (see Table 1).

#### Social mobility

Problems in the countryside and new opportunities in the cities led to a trebling of the urban population in the 1930s. Promotions were available to experienced workers and during the 1930s, the **bourgeois** specialists who had run Russian industry during the NEP were replaced by 150,000 new **red specialists**. In addition, the government invested in technical education, and workers were encouraged to attend courses at Russia's universities.

| Production (millions of tonnes) | 1928 | 1932 |
|---|---|---|
| Iron | 3.3 | 6.2 |
| Steel | 4.0 | 5.9 |
| Coal | 35.4 | 64.3 |
| Oil | 11.7 | 21.4 |

▲ Table 1

### Failures of the First Five-Year Plan

#### Quantity and quality

Production increased, but Gosplan's audacious targets were rarely met (see Table 2).

Additionally, the Plan focused on quantity rather than quality. As a result, much of what was produced was of such poor quality that it was useless. The focus on quantity, and the extreme pressure put on managers to meet targets, led to widespread lying about the extent of production.

| Production | % of target met |
|---|---|
| Iron | 78% |
| Steel | 71% |
| Coal | 95% |

▲ Table 2

#### Living standards

Life became more difficult under the First Five-Year Plan. Stalin introduced a seven-day working week and longer working hours. Lateness, striking and breaking industrial equipment were criminalised. **Consumer goods** were extremely scarce as Gosplan had prioritised heavy industry. New industrial towns, such as **Magnitogorsk**, were often little more than a collection of huts and tents with no heating or sanitation.

#### Black market

One objective of the First Five-Year Plan was to abolish the free market. However, the scarcity of consumer goods led to the development of a **black market**. **Speculators** sold vodka, cigarettes, food and footwear for extortionate prices.

#### Slave labour

Many of the successes of the First Five-Year Plan were achieved through slave labour. Peasants who had been arrested as a result of dekulakisation were sent to **labour camps** and forced to work on industrial projects. For example, 40,000 prisoners were used to build Magnitogorsk.

## Turning assertion into argument  **a**

Below are a sample exam-style question and a series of assertions. Read the question and then add a justification to each of the assertions to turn it into an argument.

**How successful was the First Five-Year Plan?**

The First Five-Year Plan was highly successful in terms of production because _____

_____

The First Five-Year Plan was more successful in terms of quantity of materials than quality of materials because _____

_____

The First Five-Year Plan did not benefit the people of Russia as much as the NEP because _____

_____

## Complex essay style

Below are a sample exam-style question, a list of key points to be made in the essay, and a simple introduction and conclusion. Read the question, the key points, and the introduction and conclusion. Rewrite the introduction and conclusion in order to develop an argument.

**How successful was the First Five-Year Plan?**

### Key points
- Success – heavy industry
- Success – social mobility
- Failure – quality of materials
- Failure – living standards
- Failure – black market
- Failure – slave labour

### Introduction

The First Five-Year Plan was a success in terms of heavy industry and social mobility. However, it was a failure in the sense that the quality of materials produced was low, living standards declined, it failed to abolish the free market, and it relied on slave labour.

### Conclusion

Overall, the First Five-Year Plan was a failure. The main way it was a failure was that the quality of materials produced was low. It also failed because living standards declined, it failed to abolish the free market, and it relied on slave labour.

## The Second Five-Year Plan 1933–38

Revised

## The changing nature of the Second Five-Year Plan

### 'Three Good Years'

Initially, the Second Five-Year Plan tried to develop the Russian economy in a more rounded way. Consequently, it stressed electrification, transport, **new industries**, **labour productivity** and consumer goods, as well as heavy industry. This change came about due to the following reasons.

- A faction of the **Politburo**, known as the **Kirov Group**, put pressure on Stalin to prioritise living standards and consumer goods. They believed that this would increase the Party's popularity. The availability of consumer goods led the Russian people to describe the period 1933 to 1936 as 'three good years'.
- During the First Five-Year Plan, large quantities of raw materials were produced but not used because there was no way of transporting them across Russia.
- The First Five-Year Plan had produced a generation of workers who were able to perform complex industrial tasks.

### Rearmament

In 1936, the priorities of the Second Five-Year Plan changed. The government scaled back spending on consumer goods in order to prioritise rearmament. This change occurred for the following reasons.

- Germany was rearming and Russian planners feared a war with **Hitler**.
- Kirov had been assassinated in 1934 and his followers had been purged in the Great Terror (see page 34).

## Successes of the Second Five-Year Plan

| Aspect of the Plan | Evidence of success |
|---|---|
| Transport | • The Moscow Metro opened in 1935 and the Volga Canal was completed by 1937. |
| Consumer goods | • Bread rationing ended in 1934.<br>• Between 1933 and 1937, production of consumer goods doubled. |
| Labour productivity | • The **Stakhanovite movement** increased labour productivity across Russian industry. |
| Heavy industry | • Steel output trebled and coal production doubled. |
| Rearmament | • Spending on rearmament rose from 4 per cent of **GDP** in 1933 to 17 per cent in 1937. |

## Failures of the Second Five-Year Plan

| Aspect of the Plan | Evidence of failure |
|---|---|
| Housing | • Many new houses lacked running water and basic sanitation.<br>• 650,000 people in Moscow had no access to a public bathhouse. |
| Consumer goods | • In spite of an increase in the availability of bread, many Russians had a poor diet.<br>• New clothing was difficult to obtain: for example, a queue of 6,000 formed outside a Leningrad shoe shop in 1934. |
| Inequalities | • 55,000 senior communists were entitled to a higher standard of living, including holiday homes, chauffeur-driven limousines and special consumer goods.<br>• Stakhanovites were entitled to large financial rewards. Alexei Stakhanov received one month's pay in one day, a new apartment, a telephone and holiday tickets. |
| Quantity and quality | • The problems of the First Five-Year Plan continued into the Second. |

## Identify an argument

Below are a series of definitions, a sample exam-style question and two sample conclusions. One of the conclusions achieves a high level because it contains an argument. The other achieves a lower level because it contains only description and assertion. Identify which is which. The mark scheme on page 3 will help you.

- **Description:** a detailed account.
- **Assertion:** a statement of fact or an opinion that is not supported by a reason.
- **Reason:** a statement that explains or justifies something.
- **Argument:** an assertion justified with a reason.

How far did the Second Five-Year Plan differ from the First Five-Year Plan?

> The Second Five-Year Plan was quite different from the First Five-Year Plan. The First Five-Year Plan focused on heavy industry, which was important to the economy as a whole. The Second Five-Year Plan developed the economy in different areas. More investment was given to consumer goods, transport and the development of new industries. However, at the end of the Second Five-Year Plan the priorities changed in favour of heavy industry and rearmament.

> The Second Five-Year Plan was significantly different from the First Five-Year Plan because for the first few years it was more realistic. It was more realistic in the sense that it recognised that workers needed incentives. This gave rise to the birth of the Stakhanovite movement. Equally, it was more realistic in the sense that planners emphasised consumer goods and living standards in a way that was not the case in the First Five-Year Plan. Finally, it was more realistic in the sense that it addressed some of the problems of the First Five-Year Plan, particularly in the area of transport. Nonetheless, this realism only lasted for the first half of the Plan, the second half reflected Stalin's priorities during the First Five-Year Plan, particularly heavy industry.

## Develop the detail

Below are a sample exam-style question and a paragraph written in answer to this question. The paragraph contains a limited amount of detail. Annotate the paragraph to add additional detail to the answer.

How successful was Stalin's economic policy in the period 1928–38?

> Stalin's economic policy was most successful during the Second Five-Year Plan. For example, transport improved. In addition, consumer goods became more widely available to Russian workers. Labour productivity also increased. There was even greater success in terms of heavy industry, and by the end of the Plan, rearmament was happening too. But there were problems. Housing and hygiene were a disaster. Diet and clothing remained poor for many workers. There were also new inequalities. In this way, the Second Five-Year Plan was much more successful than the First, but it was not a complete success because although productivity improved, the living conditions of many workers remained poor.

## The Third Five-Year Plan 1938–41

Revised

The Third Five-Year Plan continued the focus on rearmament and heavy industry. However, it was hampered by the chaos created by the Great Terror.

### Successes of the Third Five-Year Plan

| Aspect of the Plan | Evidence of success |
|---|---|
| Rearmament | • Total investment in rearmament doubled between 1938 and 1940.<br>• In 1939, nine new aircraft factories were constructed. |
| Heavy industry | • Coal production jumped from 128 million tonnes in 1937 to 166 million tonnes in 1940.<br>• Crude oil production rose from 29 million tonnes in 1937 to 31 million tonnes in 1940. |
| Worker discipline | • Internal passports were introduced to stop workers from travelling around Russia in search of higher-paid jobs. |

### Failures of the Third Five-Year Plan

| Aspect of the Plan | Evidence of failure |
|---|---|
| Administration | • Stalin's **purges** removed the most experienced economic planners and industrial managers.<br>• Due to the purges, Gosplan was never able to publish a complete version of the Plan.<br>• For these reasons, the execution of the Plan was highly chaotic. |
| Heavy industry | • Purges of industrial managers led to a stagnation in the production of steel. This remained at 18 million tonnes – the same level as under the Second Five-Year Plan. |
| Consumer goods | • Food rationing was introduced: bread, meat, pasta, sugar, fish, butter, tea, cigarettes, soap and lighter fluid were rationed.<br>• It was impossible to buy consumer goods such as refrigerators. This made it very difficult to store fresh food.<br>• By 1941, on average, there was only one shop per 476 people. |

### Russian industry by 1941

Stalin's plans transformed Russia into a highly industrialised and urbanised nation. By 1941, Russian industry could produce enormous quantities of raw materials. Nonetheless, the development of the economy had been uneven. While heavy industry had grown massively, consumer goods were scarcer than they had been under the NEP, diet was worse, and new industries producing specialist equipment grew slowly.

Crucially, by emphasising heavy industry and rearmament, Stalin had laid the foundation for victory in the Second World War, but he had done so at the expense of the living standards of the people of Russia.

RAG – Rate the timeline

Below are a sample exam-style question and a timeline. Read the question, study the timeline and, using three coloured pens, put a red, amber or green star next to the events to show:

- red – events and policies that have no relevance to the question
- amber – events and policies that have some significance to the question
- green – events and policies that are directly relevant to the question.

1. How successful was Stalin's 'revolution from above' at modernising the Russian economy in the years prior to 1941?

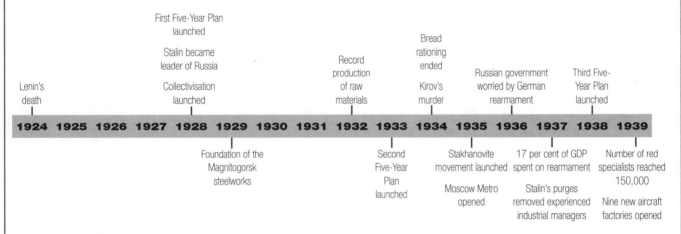

Now repeat the activity with the following questions. You could use different colours, or number your stars 1, 2 and 3.

2. Why were living standards in Russia so low in the period 1928–41?

3. Why did the priorities of the first three Five-Year Plans change over time?

 Simple essay style

Below are three sample exam questions. Use your own knowledge and the information on the opposite page to produce plans for these questions. For each plan, choose four general points, and provide three pieces of specific information to support each general point. Once you have planned each essay, write the introduction and conclusion for the essay. The introduction should list the points to be discussed in the essay. The conclusion should summarise the key points and justify which point was the most important.

How successful was Stalin's 'revolution from above' at modernising the Russian economy in the years prior to 1941?

Why were living standards in Russia so low in the period 1928–41?

Why did the priorities of the first three Five-Year Plans change over time?

Recommended reading

Below is a list of suggested further reading on this topic.

- Orlando Figes, *The Whisperers: Private Life in Stalin's Russia* (pages 148–170). Allen Lane, 2008.
- Kevin McDermott, *Stalin* (pages 64–87). Palgrave, 2006.

## The Great Retreat: women

Trotsky described the 1930s as 'the Great Retreat'. He was comparing the 1920s, a period of liberalisation in terms of attitudes to sex, the family and the role of women, to the 1930s in which more traditional attitudes were reasserted. Nonetheless, the 1930s did witness a large increase in the number of women earning money in factories and on farms.

## Women at work

The number of women working in industry increased massively between 1928 and 1941. In 1928, only 3 million women worked in Russian industry. By 1940, this figure was 13 million: 41 per cent of workers in heavy industry were women. At the same time, the government increased educational opportunities for women, and the number of women in education doubled.

Women also played a considerable role in agriculture. By 1945, 80 per cent of collective farm workers were women. In addition, there were a number of celebrated female Stakhanovites in agriculture: Pasha Angelina was well-known for organising the first Women's Tractor Brigade and Maria Demchanko was rewarded for increasing her yield of sugar beet by 400 per cent.

Nevertheless, inequalities remained in terms of pay. Women earned, on average, 40 per cent less than men.

## Women at home

In addition to working, women were expected to run the home. Indeed, women spent on average five times longer on domestic chores than men.

The domestic role of women was emphasised by the Communist Party, which expected women to resign from their jobs once they got married. Furthermore, the Communist Women's section encouraged 'wife activists' to set an example to other women by running well-ordered homes.

## Sex and babies

Traditional attitudes to sex were reasserted in 1936 when homosexuality and adultery were criminalised. Additionally, contraception and abortion were banned. At the same time, the government promoted large families. State help was available to women who had more than six children. For example, mothers with seven children received 2,000 roubles a year for five years. In the first month of this policy, 4,000 women applied for government grants, including over 2,700 who had eight children and over 1,000 who had ten or more.

## Marriage and divorce

During the 1930s, Stalin re-emphasised the importance of marriage. Wedding rings, which had been banned in 1928, were reintroduced in 1936, along with special wedding certificates that were printed on high-quality paper. At the same time, men who had affairs were named and shamed in the **Soviet** media, in publications such as the trade union newspaper, *Trud*.

Divorce was made more expensive and more complex. The cost of a first divorce was 50 roubles, approximately one week's wages. A second divorce would cost 150 roubles, and a third 300. Men who left their families were also expected to contribute 60 per cent of their income in child support.

As a result of these measures, marriage became the norm: in 1937, 91 per cent of men and 82 per cent of women in their thirties were married.

## Support or challenge?

Below is a sample exam-style question, which asks how far you agree with a specific statement. Below this are a series of general statements that are relevant to the question. Using your own knowledge and the information on the opposite page, decide whether these statements support or challenge the statement in the question and tick the appropriate box.

'Stalin's social policy was a "Great Retreat" for the Soviet people.' How far do you agree with this statement?

| | SUPPORT | CHALLENGE |
|---|---|---|
| Women were rewarded for having large families. | | |
| The laws regarding contraception changed. | | |
| The laws regarding abortion changed. | | |
| The laws regarding homosexuality changed. | | |
| The laws regarding divorce changed. | | |
| Women were paid for working in industry. | | |
| Many women worked on collective farms. | | |
| Women joined the Stakhanovite movement. | | |

## Eliminate irrelevance

Below are a sample exam-style question and a paragraph written in answer to this question. Read the paragraph and identify parts that are not directly relevant to the question. Draw a line through the information that is irrelevant and justify your deletions in the margin.

How far did Stalinism create sexual equality in Russia in the period 1928–41?

Stalinism did lead to greater sexual equality in the world of work. In the period 1928–41, the number of women employed in industry rose from 3 million to over 13 million. This could be because of the Five-Year Plans, which aimed to transform Russia from an agricultural economy to an industrial one. What is more, the number of women employed on collective farms also increased and a number of women, such as Pasha Angelina and Maria Demchanko, became national celebrities as successful members of the Stakhanovite movement. Even so, women were still not fully equal. On farms, conditions were dreadful because of dekulakisation and the Great Famine. Also, even in 1940, women only accounted for 41 per cent of workers in heavy industry and on average they earned around 40 per cent less than men. In this way, greater sexual equality was achieved in the workplace, but full sexual equality was not achieved because wage differences suggest women's work was not valued as highly as that of men.

## The Great Retreat: family and education

### Family

Soviet propaganda emphasised the importance of the family.

- The working class was described as 'one big family' with Stalin as its father.
- Stalin was presented as a family man following a highly publicised visit to his aging mother in his hometown of Tbilisi.
- Propaganda demonised men who cheated on their wives and neglected their families.

### Education

#### Komsomol

**Komsomol** was the Soviet youth organisation. Its goal was to turn Soviet children into hardworking and obedient citizens. *Komsomolskaia Pravda*, the youth newspaper, instructed children to respect and love their parents. The newspaper told the story of Pavlik Morozov, a member of Komsomol, who had been murdered by a kulak at the age of fourteen. Morozov was presented as the perfect child, devoted to Stalin and his family.

In keeping with conservative morality of the 1930s, Komsomol promoted sexual abstinence amongst young people. This advice was backed up by 'medical virginity checks' performed on young women by senior figures on collective farms. Additionally, the police were empowered to arrest young women who dressed in a revealing manner.

#### School

In 1935, Stalin introduced a new curriculum. Education in the 1920s had stressed freedom of thought. By contrast, education in the 1930s focused on discipline, national tradition, literacy and numeracy. The aim of school was to produce disciplined and educated workers, who were ready to work in industry and contribute to the fulfilment of the Five-Year Plans.

The curriculum's core subjects were reading, writing and science. According to the new curriculum, 30 per cent of school time was devoted to Russian language and literature, 20 per cent to maths, 15 per cent to science and 10 per cent to history.

The teaching of history is a good example of Stalin's approach to education. Russia before the revolution was described as 'a prison of the peoples' and the communists were described as Russia's liberators. There was a new focus on great Russian leaders, including Ivan the Terrible and Peter the Great. Students were also taught why the communist system was better than any other in the world.

#### Teachers

The Stakhanovite movement influenced schools. Some teachers set themselves audacious targets and were rewarded for meeting them. For example, Olga Fedorovna Leonova pledged that all of her students would gain excellent grades. Her success was celebrated in the Soviet media.

The spirit of the purges was also evident in the classroom. If students failed to achieve highly, the blame was placed on teachers. The First Russian Educational Conference, held in 1939, blamed falling standards on lazy teachers who failed to plan their lessons properly, rather than on the new curriculum or the textbooks published to support it.

## Mind Map

Use the information on the opposite page to add detail to the mind map below.

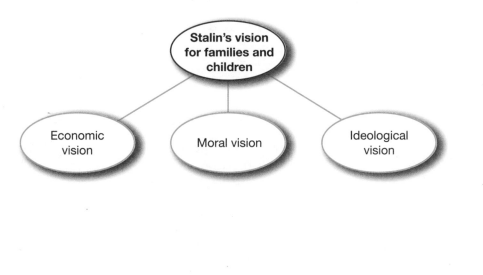

## Complex essay style

Below are a sample exam-style question, a list of key points to be made in the essay, and a simple introduction and conclusion for the essay. Read the question, the key points, and the introduction and conclusion. Rewrite the introduction and conclusion in order to develop an argument.

How far did Stalin transform the lives of women and children in the period 1928–41?

### Key points

- Women – work
- Women – home life
- Women – relationships
- Children – Komsomol
- Children – school

### Introduction

Stalin transformed the lives of women and children to a great extent. He changed the lives of women in terms of work, home life and relationships. In addition, he changed the lives of children through Komsomol and at school.

### Conclusion

Overall, Stalin transformed the lives of women and children to a great extent. He transformed the lives of women, both at home and at work, and by changing laws regarding relationships. He also changed children's school and leisure time.

## Exam focus

Below is a sample A-grade essay. Read the essay and the examiner's comments around it.

**How successful was Stalin's economic policy in the years 1928–41?**

The introduction indicates that this essay will take a thematic approach to the question, considering the key aspects of Stalin's economic policy, rather than taking collectivisation and each Five-Year Plan in turn.

Stalin's economic policy was partially successful in the years 1928–41. There was success and failure in agriculture, heavy industry, living standards, rearmament and labour productivity.

This paragraph contains a great deal of data and effectively considers the successes and failures of agriculture.

Stalin's agricultural policy was not very successful. It did succeed in the sense that by 1941, all the farms in Russia had collectivised. This meant that Stalin achieved his goal of ending the free market in agriculture, which had been established with the NEP. However, it failed in the sense that collectivisation never produced as much grain as the NEP. For example, the harvest of 1933 was 10 million tonnes less than the harvest of 1926. There were also problems with the implementation of collectivisation. Rather than collectivise, farmers tended to destroy their crops and animals. For example, between 1929 and 1933, 18 million horses and 10 million sheep and goats were killed. The clearest evidence of failure was the famine between 1932 and 1934, which resulted in the deaths of 10 million people. In this way, Stalin's agricultural policy was largely unsuccessful because although full collectivisation was achieved, it resulted in a huge decline in production.

This paragraph considers the whole period specified in the question by dealing with all three Five-Year Plans.

Stalin's biggest success was in terms of heavy industry. The first three of Stalin's Five-Year Plans focused on heavy industry. Under the First Five-Year Plan, production of iron, coal and oil almost doubled and production of steel rose significantly from 4 million tonnes in 1928 to almost 6 million tonnes in 1932. Similarly, steel output trebled under the Second Five-Year Plan, and coal output doubled. The Third Five-Year Plan also saw an increase in coal production of 38 million tonnes and an increase in the production of crude oil of 2 million tonnes. Nonetheless, while large amounts were produced, the quality of production was often poor. What is more, despite the increase in production, Stalin's targets were rarely met. Clearly, although industry was successful in terms of quantity, it was less successful in terms of quality and fulfilling Stalin's targets.

The government's emphasis on living standards changed over time. This paragraph makes that explicit, allowing for more sophisticated analysis.

The Five-Year Plans failed to improve the living standards of the Russian people. During the First Five-Year Plan, Russians were required to work a seven-day week. Food, including bread, was rationed and consumer goods, such as vodka, cigarettes and footwear, were only really available on the black market. Under pressure from the Kirov Group, the Second Five-Year Plan initially increased the amount of consumer goods produced. For example, bread rationing ended in 1934, and during the course of the Plan, the production of consumer goods doubled. Even so, once rearmament started in 1936, the production of consumer goods declined significantly. In addition, most Russians lived on a poor diet. Living standards were a failure of Stalin's economic policy because, with the exception of 'three good years' living standards were poorer than they had been before Stalin's policies were introduced.

Rearmament was a success for Stalin's economic policy. Rearmament started in 1936 and by 1937, the government's armament budget had risen to 17 per cent of GDP, from only 4 per cent in 1933. Further successes were achieved in the Third Five-Year Plan. Total investment in rearmament doubled in the first two years of the Plan. In addition, nine new aircraft factories were constructed in 1939. However, there were problems with rearmament. Stalin's Great Terror caused chaos in Gosplan, which meant that the Third Five-Year Plan was not administered very efficiently. Rearmament was a success because of the massive increase in investment, but it could have been more successful if Gosplan had been more organised.

Labour productivity became more successful under the Second Five-Year Plan. In the First Five-Year Plan, Russian workers worked seven days a week but did not work very efficiently. The Stakhanovite movement, which started during the Second Five-Year Plan, increased labour productivity by offering rewards to Russian workers. Alexei Stakhanov, for example, received one month's pay, a new apartment and holiday tickets for mining a record amount of coal in one shift. His example motivated other Stakhanovites such as Pasha Angelina, who organised the first Women's Tractor Brigade, and Maria Demchanko, who increased her yield of sugar beet by 400 per cent. Labour productivity was a success of Stalin's economic policy because the Stakhanovite movement, which influenced both industry and agriculture, inspired workers to produce more.

In conclusion, Stalin's economic policy was partially successful because while the quantity of production in heavy industry increased and the amount of investment in armament also increased, living standards and agricultural production did not. There were other successes in areas like labour productivity, but overall the plans did not improve the living and working conditions of the Russian people.

This paragraph extends the range of the essay, moving beyond production to consider productivity.

24/30

This is a well-focused essay, which includes a large amount of relevant detail. Every single paragraph presents a coherent analysis of the factor it discusses. Nevertheless, this essay cannot enter Level 5 because the introduction and conclusion simply summarise the essay without developing an argument.

## Moving from Level 4 to Level 5

The exam focus at the end of Section 1 provided a Level 5 essay. The essay here achieves a Level 4. Read both essays, and the examiner's comments provided. Make a list of the additional features required to push a Level 4 essay into Level 5.

# Section 3:
## Persecution and control – the totalitarian regime

## Causes of the Great Terror

Between 1936 and 1938, Russia experienced the Great Terror. Using the secret police, Stalin persecuted all those he believed to be a threat to his regime. More than 10 million people died.

### Lenin's police state

The Great Terror was carried out by the **NKVD**. Lenin had used the secret police against his political enemies. Stalin gave them a new role: he turned the NKVD against the **Communist** Party, the last institution that could oppose his **personal rule**.

### Stalin's paranoia

Stalin was aware that Trotsky, Zinoviev, Kamenev and Bukharin had all held leading positions in the Communist Party before falling from power. Stalin was worried that he would suffer the same fate. He feared opposition from groups loyal to his former rivals.

- The **Red Army** had been established by Trotsky, his archrival, and many soldiers were loyal to their former leader.
- Moscow and **Leningrad** had been the powerbases of Zinoviev and Kamenev.
- Genrikh Yagoda, Head of the NKVD, had sided with Bukharin in 1928.

### Economics

- Stalin needed a scapegoat for the failings of the Five-Year Plans. He blamed 'wreckers', who were publically tried and punished.
- Stalin needed a large labour force to construct projects such as **Magnitogorsk**. Those arrested during the Terror were sent to **gulags** where they worked as slaves.

### The Congress of Victors 1934

The Seventeenth **Party Congress** was held in 1934. The vote taken at the end of the Congress to elect the new **Central Committee** was a massive upset for Stalin. Stalin came second to Kirov, receiving only 927 votes to Kirov's 1,225. Stalin was already concerned about Kirov because Kirov had forced Stalin to change his economic policy during the Second Five-Year Plan.

Following the vote, a group of senior **Bolsheviks** approached Kirov and urged him to stand against Stalin as **General Secretary**. Kirov refused, and the results were hushed up. However, the results confirmed Stalin's suspicions that many in the Party wanted a new leader.

### Kirov's murder 1934

At the end of 1934, Kirov was assassinated in Leningrad by a lone gunman. Stalin used this as a pretext to arrest his former rivals, Zinoviev and Kamenev, along with their closest followers. More generally, Stalin argued that Kirov's murder was evidence of a widespread conspiracy within the Communist Party to overthrow his government and to restore **capitalism** to Russia. Kirov's murder was the trigger for the Great Terror.

## Spot the mistake

Below are a sample exam-style question and a paragraph written in answer to this question. Why does this paragraph not get into Level 4? Once you have identified the mistake, rewrite the paragraph so that it displays the qualities of Level 4. The mark scheme on page 3 will help you.

**Why did Stalin launch the Great Terror?**

One reason that Stalin launched the Great Terror was because he was paranoid. He believed he was surrounded by people who wanted to overthrow him. He didn't trust the army. He didn't trust the NKVD either. Finally, he didn't trust many within the Communist Party. Stalin launched the Great Terror because it would allow him to purge the Party of people he did not trust, which in Stalin's case was a lot of people.

## Spectrum of significance

Below are a sample exam-style question and a list of general points that could be used to answer the question. Use your own knowledge and the information on the opposite page to reach a judgement about the importance of these general points to the question posed. Write numbers on the spectrum below to indicate their relative importance. Having done this, write a brief justification of your placement, explaining why some of these factors are more important than others. The resulting diagram could form the basis of an essay plan.

**How far do you agree that Kirov's murder was the main cause of the Great Terror?**

1. Lenin's police state
2. Stalin's paranoia
3. The need to find a scapegoat for economic failings
4. To provide slave labourers
5. The Congress of Victors
6. Kirov's murder

Very important ←——————————————————————→ Less important

## Moscow show trials

Terror raged across Russia for two years following Kirov's murder. The most public manifestation of the Great Terror were the three Moscow **show trials**, which finally dealt with Stalin's old adversaries.

## The show trials

| Show trial | Key defendants | Details |
|---|---|---|
| Trial of the Sixteen 1936 | Zinoviev Kamenev | • Zinoviev and Kamenev were charged with the murder of Kirov, plotting to disrupt Stalin's economic policy, working with foreign powers, plotting to murder Stalin and conspiring with Trotsky to restore capitalism to Russia.<br>• Zinoviev and Kamenev confessed, believing that Stalin would pardon them once the trial was over.<br>• At the conclusion of the trial, Zinoviev and Kamenev were executed.<br>• The judge summed up the trial with the words 'Shoot the mad dogs, every last one of them!' |
| Trial of the Seventeen 1937 | Trotsky (*though absent*) | • Trotsky and his supporters were charged with the same crimes as Zinoviev and Kamenev.<br>• Following torture, all defendants confessed.<br>• However, the NKVD made several mistakes, and therefore the confessions did not stand up to scrutiny. For example, one of the defendants confessed to murdering Kirov despite the fact that he was in an NKVD prison at the time of the murder.<br>• The majority of the defendants were executed. Four defendants were sent to **labour camps**.<br>• Trotsky was sentenced to death, but was in exile in Mexico and so the sentence could not be carried out. |
| Trial of the Twenty-One 1938 | Bukharin Yagoda | • Again, the defendants were charged with the same crimes as Zinoviev and Kamenev.<br>• Bukharin was charged with the additional crime of plotting to murder Lenin.<br>• Bukharin confessed to 'political responsibility' for most of the crimes as Stalin threatened to execute his wife and child if he refused.<br>• Bukharin refused to confess to plotting to murder Lenin.<br>• The defendants, including Bukharin, were executed following the trial. |

## The secret trial 1937

The trial of eight generals in 1937 was kept top secret. Stalin did not trust the leadership of the Red Army, but with war looming, he did not want to alarm the public by saying so openly. The eight generals were accused of plotting against Stalin and, following brutal torture at the hands of the NKVD, they confessed. Over the next 18 months, 34,000 soldiers were purged from the army.

## The significance of the show trials

The show trials were significant for four reasons.

- They finally removed Stalin's rivals from the 1920s.
- They silenced the people who knew the truth about **Lenin's *Testament***, and Lenin's critical judgement of Stalin.
- They removed from power people who had been appointed by Lenin, and therefore had authority independently of Stalin.
- They acted as a form of propaganda, 'proving' to the Russian people that Stalin alone could be trusted with the future of Russia.

Below are a sample exam-style question and a paragraph written in answer to this question. The paragraph contains specific examples and a concluding explanatory link back to the question, but lacks a focused first sentence. Complete the paragraph by adding this first sentence in the space provided.

**How far do you agree that the main aim of the Great Terror was to eliminate Stalin's former rivals?**

_____

_____

For example, the Trial of the Sixteen in 1936 eliminated Zinoviev and Kamenev and their key supporters from the Moscow and Leningrad Parties. The second trial — The Trial of the Seventeen — in 1937, targeted those who had supported Trotsky during the 1920s. Trotsky himself was tried and found guilty at this trial, even though he was not present. The final trial was against Bukharin and those who had supported the right wing in the last phase of the leadership struggle, including Yagoda who had initially backed Bukharin after the Duumvirate split. In this way, the Great Terror clearly eliminated Stalin's former rivals because the three Moscow show trials resulted in the conviction of the leading figures who had opposed Stalin in the 1920s.

Below are a sample exam-style question and a paragraph written in answer to this question. Read the paragraph and identify parts that are not directly relevant to the question. Draw a line through the information that is irrelevant and justify your deletions in the margin.

**How far do you agree that the main aim of the Great Terror was to eliminate Stalin's former rivals?**

One of Stalin's aims for the Great Terror was to gain greater control of the Red Army. The Red Army was a powerful and disciplined fighting force that could have been used to overthrow Stalin. Stalin was paranoid and, in the case of the Red Army, there was good reason for his paranoia. The Red Army was established and run for many years by his archrival Trotsky, who would be assassinated in Mexico in 1940. Evidence of Stalin's concern about the army is found in the secret trial of eight generals in 1937. This was not the first time Stalin had turned against Trotsky's allies, as he had turned against Zinoviev and Kamenev in 1927 after the Fifteenth Party Congress. Having found the generals guilty of treason, Stalin purged a further 34,000 soldiers from the army. Clearly, one of Stalin's aims for the Great Terror was to gain better control of the army because he could not count on its support for his leadership.

## *Yezhovshchina*

After the Trial of the Sixteen, Yagoda was replaced as Head of the NKVD by Nicolai Yezhov. Yezhov took the Great Terror to a whole new level, reforming the NKVD and extending the Terror to all areas of the country. This period was popularly known as ***Yezhovshchina***.

## The doctrine of sharpening class struggle 1937

Stalin justified the Terror with a new **doctrine**. He argued that the closer Russia came to communism, the harder the capitalists would fight. This doctrine justified increasing repression. The doctrine became official Communist Party policy at a meeting of the Central Committee in March 1937. Within three months, 70 per cent of those present at the meeting had fallen victim to the Terror, which they themselves had voted to extend.

## Conveyor belt system

Yezhov reformed the NKVD to make it more efficient. He did this in the following ways.

- He purged the NKVD itself, replacing old agents who were loyal to the Communist Party and who opposed widespread Terror, with new agents who were prepared to torture Communist Party members. In total, 23,000 members of the NKVD were executed.
- He introduced a conveyor belt system where agents worked in teams around the clock to torture suspects until they confessed.
- In collaboration with Stalin, he set targets for the numbers of arrests and executions to speed up the Terror.

## The wider Terror

The Moscow show trials were the most obvious part of the Terror. Outside Moscow, the Terror took a variety of forms.

- Inspired by the Moscow show trials, workers imprisoned their managers and put them on trial before the entire factory workforce. For example, in Yaroslavl, the managers of a rubber factory were put on trial, found guilty, and handed over to the NKVD.
- The NKVD also targeted industrial managers and government administrators. Some apartment blocks in major cities became entirely deserted as all their residents were arrested.
- In Kazan, local people put communist officials on trial for living luxurious lifestyles on public funds.
- In other areas, people also turned against the Communist Party, denouncing local officials to the NKVD as 'enemies of the people'. Between 1934 and 1938, 330,000 Party members were arrested and convicted.

## Final victims of the Terror

The Great Terror came to an end in the middle of 1938. However, there were two final victims. First, at the end of 1938, Yezhov himself was arrested. Two years later he was executed for terrorism, collaborating with other countries and moral degeneracy. He was replaced as Head of the NKVD by Lavrenti Beria, who, in 1940, masterminded the murder of Trotsky. Trotsky was killed by an NKVD agent while in exile in Mexico.

**Identify an argument**

Below are a series of definitions, a sample exam-style question and two sample conclusions. One of the conclusions achieves a high level because it contains an argument. The other achieves a lower level because it contains only a description and an assertion. Identify which is which. The mark scheme on page 3 will help you.

- **Description:** a detailed account.
- **Assertion:** a statement of fact or an opinion that is not supported by a reason.
- **Reason:** a statement that explains or justifies something.
- **Argument:** an assertion justified with a reason.

How far do you agree that members of the Communist Party were the main victims of the Great Terror?

Overall, communists were among the victims of the Great Terror. Stalin relied on the Central Committee to agree to his doctrine of sharpening class struggle. The doctrine justified launching a new wave of Terror across Russia. The Central Committee voted in favour of Stalin's proposals. However, by June 1937, many of the Central Committee of the Communist Party had become victims of the Terror. Outside Moscow, Communist Party members were also targeted. Local people resented their luxurious lifestyles, and in places like Kazan, they organised local show trials.

In conclusion, Communist Party members were the main victims of the Great Terror because they posed the greatest threat to Stalin. The Moscow show trials of 1936, 1937 and 1938 explicitly targeted the Communist Party's most senior members, as did the purge of the Central Committee in 1937. Outside of the capital, the picture was less clear as industrial managers, who were not necessarily members of the Communist Party, were also caught up in the purges. Even so, the example of the town of Kazan indicates that local people used the opportunity of the Terror to turn against the Party. Evidently, Stalin's goal was to rid the Party of his rivals, and the goal of local people was to punish corrupt communists. As a result, in both ways, Communist Party members were the main victims of the Great Terror.

 **Turning assertion into argument**

Below are a sample exam-style question and two assertions. Read the question and then add a justification to each of the assertions to turn it into an argument.

How far do you agree that members of the Communist Party were the main victims of the Great Terror between 1936 and 1938?

Terror escalated massively under Yezhov because

_____

_____

Outside Moscow, factory managers, rather than Communist Party members, can be considered the main victims of the Great Terror because

_____

_____

## The impact of the Terror

Revised

The consequences of the Terror were wide-ranging, affecting Russia's economy, politics and society.

## Economic consequences

- The removal of Kirov's supporters from the **Politburo** allowed Stalin to change the direction of the Second Five-Year Plan in 1936.
- In order to escape the wrath of the NKVD, industrial managers lied about their production figures.
- **Purges** of **Gosplan** meant that the Third Five-Year Plan was never published. This led to further confusion in industry.
- The removal of local managers reduced the efficiency of Russia's industry. For example, in the Donbas region of the Ukraine, coal production, which had trebled between 1928 and 1936, stagnated for the duration of the Terror.

## Political consequences

### The consolidation of Stalin's power

- The Moscow show trials removed Stalin's rivals from the 1920s.
- The removal of Kirov's supporters eliminated those who wanted to moderate some aspects of Stalin's policies.
- Stalin was able to deflect criticism of his economic policy by accusing others of sabotaging the Five-Year Plans.

### The Communist Party

- The administration of Russian government ground to a halt as communist officials were so scared of being purged that they stopped making decisions.
- Junior members of the Communist Party, who were more loyal to Stalin, were promoted as their bosses were purged.

## Social consequences

### Family life

The Terror had a significant impact on family life.

- Approximately 10 per cent of adult males fell victim to the Terror.
- 95 per cent of those arrested were men, the majority of whom were aged between 30 and 45 and were husbands and fathers.
- The children of those arrested were persecuted and humiliated at school and in **Komsomol**.

### Escaping the Terror

There were a variety of ways of escaping the Terror. One key way was to become a member of the **working class**.

- People at risk of being purged moved away from their hometowns and took on new identities as industrial workers. This was not always successful. For example, Vladimir Gromov took on a new identity as a prize-winning architect and engineer. After receiving a payment of 1 million roubles by the government, he was exposed as a fraud and sentenced to ten years in a gulag.
- The daughters of victims of the Terror attempted to begin new lives by marrying members of the working class.
- Some local officials could be bribed to issue new identity papers establishing a new working-class identity.

### The Terror from below

Ordinary people who were dissatisfied with life in Stalin's Russia used the Terror to express their frustration and promote their own interests.

- Stakhanovites played a leading role in the Terror and used it as an opportunity to remove their managers and gain promotion.
- Unscrupulous workers would inform on their neighbours and colleagues in order to get the properties that were vacated as a result of the purges.

## Delete as applicable

Below are a sample exam-style question and a paragraph written in answer to this question. Read the paragraph and decide which option (in bold) is most appropriate. Delete the least appropriate options and complete the paragraph by justifying your selection.

### How widespread was the Great Terror between 1936 and 1938?

The Great Terror was **extremely widespread/moderately widespread/limited in scope** between 1937 and 1938. For example, the people of Russia described 1937 and 1938 as 'Yezhovshchina', meaning that the Terror affected all aspects of people's lives. Some groups of people, such as industrial managers and government administrators, were ruthlessly targeted. Indeed, there were some apartment blocks in Moscow that were deserted by 1938 as all of their residents had been arrested. However, some groups were not directly affected by the Terror. Only 5 per cent of the Terror's victims were women. Similarly, members of the Stakhanovite movement and workers in their twenties were much less likely to be targeted. In this way, the Great Terror between 1937 and 1938 was **extremely widespread/moderately widespread/limited in scope** because

_____

_____

## You're the examiner

Below are a sample exam-style question and a paragraph written in answer to this question. Read the paragraph and the mark scheme provided on page 3. Decide which level you would award the paragraph. Write the level below, along with a justification for your decision.

### How far is it accurate to state that the main consequence of the Great Terror was the consolidation of Stalin's personal power?

Stalin was keen to make sure that he was in charge and that no one else could challenge him. That is why he made the show trials, which removed people like Zinoviev and Bukharin, who had been important in the Party. For example, there was the Trial of the Sixteen in 1936, the Trial of the Seventeen in 1937, and the Trial of the Twenty-One in 1938. Zinoviev and Bukharin, and Trotsky as well, had tried to win the leadership of the Party after Lenin's death. Zinoviev and Trotsky made the United Opposition and Bukharin made the Right Opposition to challenge Stalin. Stalin never forgave them for this and when he had the chance he convicted them and killed them.

Level:    Reason for choosing this level:

_____

_____

## Socialist Realism

Art in the 1920s was revolutionary in the sense that it was abstract, consisting of geometric shapes rather than pictures of landscapes or people. Stalin, however, wanted art that would inspire the workers and celebrate his economic achievements. As a result, a new artistic style was born – **Socialist Realism**.

### Defining Socialist Realism

There were two aspects to Socialist Realism. First, the art needed to reflect **socialist** values. Secondly, it needed to be realistic in a traditional sense. In painting, realism meant that works of art should look photographic; in literature, it meant stories that described the lives of working people; and in architecture, it meant focusing on traditional, classical styles.

## The impact of Socialist Realism

Socialist Realism was designed to show the achievements of Stalin's Russia and to give an inspiring glimpse of what could be achieved in years to come. Socialist Realism was a form of social control, and therefore an important part of Stalin's **totalitarian** regime, because it persuaded workers and peasants that the sacrifices that they were making were part of a grand vision and would lead to a better future for the people of Russia. In this way, Stalin used art to maintain the popularity of the regime and consolidate his own position.

## Examples of Socialist Realism

### Painting

| Work/artist | Date | Details |
|---|---|---|
| *Voting to Expel the Kulak from the Collective Farm* (S. Y. Adlivankin) | 1931 | Shows a row of happy **peasants** voting to remove a mean-looking kulak from their farm. |
| *Training Cadets for Magnitogorsk* (A. V. Lobanov) | 1932 | Depicts cadets being trained in methods of industrial production prior to undertaking work at Magnitogorsk. |
| *Leader, Teacher, Friend* (G. Shegal) | 1935 | Shows Stalin speaking to peasants at the Second Congress of Collective Farm Workers. |

### Literature

| Work/author | Date | Details |
|---|---|---|
| *Forward, Oh Time* (Valentine Kataev) | 1934 | Describes the excitement of working at a steel factory during the Second Five-Year Plan. |
| *Quiet Flows the Don* (M. A. Sholokhov) | 1934 | A love story, describing the relationship of two Russian peasants, who are caught up in the fight to establish communism in Russia. |
| *How the Steel was Tempered* (Nikolai Ostrovsky) | 1936 | Tells the story of a Russian worker who joins the Red Army and fights in the **Russian Civil War**. |

### Architecture

| Work/location | Date | Details |
|---|---|---|
| Teatralnaya, Moscow | 1935 | Moscow Metro station. Designed to look like a palace, and yet accessible to workers. |
| Palace of the Soviets, Moscow | 1936 | Designed to be the tallest building in the world, with a statue of Lenin at its pinnacle. It was never built as the design was too expensive. |
| Theatre of the Red Army, Moscow | 1938 | Built in the shape of a five-point communist star. The interior of the building is decorated with murals glorifying the Red Army. |

## Support or challenge?

Below is a sample exam-style question that asks how far you agree with a specific statement. Below this are a series of general statements that are relevant to the question. Using your own knowledge and the information on the opposite page, decide whether these statements support or challenge the statement in the question and tick the appropriate box.

'Stalin created a totalitarian regime during the 1930s.' How far do you agree with this statement?

| | SUPPORT | CHALLENGE |
|---|---|---|
| The Great Terror removed Stalin's rivals from the Party. | | |
| Socialist Realism was introduced. | | |
| The Kirov Group reformed the Second Five-Year Plan. | | |
| The laws regarding homosexuality changed. | | |
| Yezhov reformed the NKVD. | | |
| Industrial managers lied about meeting targets. | | |
| The Central Committee agreed the doctrine of sharpening class struggle. | | |
| **Collectivisation** was halted in 1930. | | |

## Develop the detail   ⓐ

Below are a sample exam-style question and a paragraph written in answer to this question. The paragraph contains a limited amount of detail. Annotate the paragraph to add additional detail to the answer.

How far do you agree that art was the main form of social control in Russia in the 1930s?

Art was a significant form of social control in Russia in the 1930s. Stalin introduced a new form of art called Socialist Realism. There were Socialist Realist paintings showing happy workers and peasants, Socialist Realist literature celebrating the successes of Stalin's policies, and Socialist Realist architecture creating grand places for workers. All of these forms of art acted as a form of social control because they promoted communist values and inspired workers to support the regime.

## Cult of Personality

The Cult of Stalin served an important purpose in Stalin's totalitarian regime. The celebration of Stalin's genius and goodness allowed people to feel loyalty and gratitude to Stalin himself, even when the regime failed them.

## Official histories

The Cult of Stalin was underpinned by official histories that exaggerated Stalin's role during the **October Revolution** and his closeness with Lenin, and ridiculed his former opponents. The two most important histories of this kind were:

■ *A Short Course of the History of the All Union Communist Party* (1939)

■ *Joseph Stalin: A Short Biography* (1947).

## Faking history

History was also rewritten by doctoring photographs and creating paintings and films that presented a false picture of the past. For example, photographs showing Trotsky and Lenin together were altered to remove Trotsky from the picture. Similarly, paintings, such as *Stalin as an Organiser of the October Revolution* by Karp Trokhimenko (1945), showed Stalin playing the leading role in planning the October Revolution. In reality, this role had been played by Trotsky.

## Stalin in art

### Lenin's pupil

In the 1930s, Socialist Realist art presented Stalin as Lenin's pupil. In this sense, Stalin was presented as faithfully carrying on the work that Lenin had started. For example, the photomontage *Long Live the Stalinist Order of Heroes and Stakhanovites* by Gustavs Klucis (1936) shows Stalin standing in front of a bust of Lenin, symbolising the fact that Stalin was 'the Lenin of today'.

### The myth of the two leaders

By the late 1930s, **Soviet** history had been rewritten again. Lenin's role was slightly reduced while Stalin's was further increased. According to the myth of the two leaders, Stalin had always been Lenin's equal, and the two men, rather than Lenin alone, had led the October Revolution. For example, Mikhail Romm's film *Lenin in October* (1937) depicted Stalin at Lenin's side continually throughout the Revolution. Finally, in the late 1930s, Marxism-Leninism, which had been the official ideology of the Soviet Union, became known as Marxism-Leninism-Stalinism, indicating that Stalin was now considered an equal of Lenin and Marx.

### The popular cult

The Cult of Stalin, and the continuing Cult of Lenin, provided a focus for popular enthusiasm about communism. For example, Stalin's birthday became a national holiday, marked by celebrations across Russia. Equally, the Cult of Lenin, which focused on Lenin's tomb in Moscow, replaced traditional Christian symbolism with a new, communist symbolism. All citizens could participate in the cults by buying paintings or sculptures of Lenin and Stalin or collections of their speeches.

---

### The significance of the Cult of Personality

The **Cult of Personality** was significant because it emphasised the wisdom and greatness of Stalin, leader of Russia. Russian people felt that the destiny of their country was in safe hands because Stalin was an infallible leader who was carrying on the work on Lenin, a man who had been turned into a secular saint.

---

## Mind Map

Use the information in Sections 2 and 3 to add detail to the mind map below.

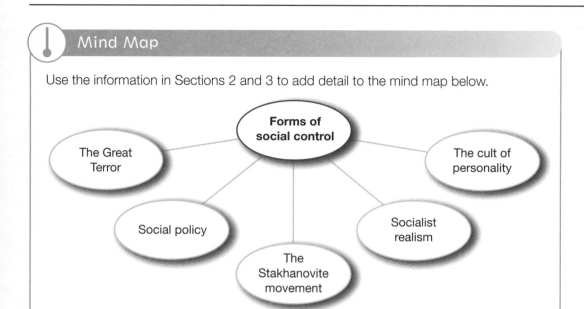

## Complex essay style

Below are a sample exam-style question, a list of key points to be made in the essay, and a simple introduction and conclusion for the essay. Read the question, the key points, and the introduction and conclusion. Rewrite the introduction and the conclusion in order to develop an argument.

> To what extent was the Great Terror Stalin's main form of social control during the 1930s?

### Key points

- The Great Terror
- Social policy
- The Stakhanovite movement
- Socialist Realism
- The Cult of Personality

### Introduction

*There were five key ways in which Stalin controlled society during the 1930s. These were the Great Terror, social policy, the Stakhanovite movement, Socialist Realism and the Cult of Personality.*

### Conclusion

*In conclusion, Stalin controlled society in five main ways: the Great Terror, social policy, the Stakhanovite movement, Socialist Realism and the Cult of Personality. The most significant of these was the Great Terror.*

## Recommended reading

Below is a list of suggested further reading on this topic.

- Orlando Figes, *The Whisperers: Private Life in Stalin's Russia* (pages 227–251). Allen Lane, 2008.
- Donald Rayfield, *Stalin and his Hangmen* (pages 143–163). Penguin, 2005.
- Arthur Koestler, *Darkness at Noon*. Vintage, 2007.

## Exam focus

Below is a sample A-grade essay. Read the essay and the examiner's comments around it.

**How far do you agree that Stalin's totalitarian regime was supported mainly by the Cult of Personality?**

The essay begins with a clear definition of totalitarianism.

The introduction evaluates the relative significance of the different factors in terms of their ability to inspire total commitment and their ability to create total control. This is linked to a clear definition of totalitarianism.

Stalin's totalitarian regime, which emerged in the 1930s, was based on many factors. The Cult of Personality, the Great Terror, Socialist Realism and Stalin's social and economic policy all played their part in sustaining a totalitarian regime; that is, a regime that aimed at total control and demanded total commitment from all its citizens. Overall, the Cult of Personality played an important role in that it helped to inspire loyalty, but other factors were more important in terms of extending control.

This paragraph uses two very detailed examples to support its point.

Stalin's Cult of Personality was an important aspect of his totalitarian regime. Totalitarianism requires not just obedience but total commitment to the regime. The Cult of Personality inspired total commitment by turning Stalin into a 'leader, teacher, friend.' While it was difficult to feel love for the Communist Party or the Five-Year Plans, the Cult of Personality allowed people to feel love towards Stalin, which inspired them to be loyal to the regime. The Cult of Personality was established in paintings such as 'Long Live the Stalinist Order of Heroes and Stakhanovites' (1936), which showed Stalin celebrating with workers and communists. Another example is Mikhail Romm's film 'Lenin in October' (1937) which presented Stalin as Lenin's equal and therefore emphasised that Stalin was 'the Lenin of today'. Clearly, the Cult of Personality was key support for Stalin's totalitarian regime because works of art inspired people to love Stalin and therefore support the regime.

The first sentence links back to the definition of totalitarianism given in the introduction.

The paragraph concludes by clearly explaining how the Terror helped support totalitarianism.

The Great Terror helped build a totalitarian regime by extending Stalin's control and inspiring loyalty. The three Moscow show trials of 1936, 1937 and 1938 extended Stalin's control by first removing Zinoviev and Kamenev, secondly removing Trotsky's key supporters, and lastly by removing Bukharin. It also inspired loyalty as it allowed people at a local level, particularly Stakhanovites, to rise up against their bosses and corrupt Party members, following Stalin's example, and remove them from their positions. For example, in Kazan, local people put communist officials on trial for using public funds to finance their luxurious lifestyles. In this way, the Great Terror helped extend Stalin's control by removing his old enemies, and inspired loyalty by allowing people to find scapegoats for their discontent.

Socialist Realism was another important support for Stalin's totalitarianism because it inspired loyalty. The painting 'Voting to Expel the Kulak from the Collective Farm' (1931) turned the persecution of the kulaks into a heroic act. Equally, the painting 'Training Cadets for Magnitogorsk' (1932) turned a normal meeting in a factory into a heroic victory for the working class. Finally, the 1934 novel 'Forward, Oh Time', by Valentine Kataev celebrated the production of steel, a crucial aspect of Stalin's economic policy. In this way, Socialist Realism helped create a totalitarian regime by producing inspirational art that celebrated the everyday life of Russia's citizens.

Again, this paragraph uses specific titles, dates, and the name of an author to support its comments about Socialist Realism.

Economic and social policies were also key to Stalin's totalitarianism. Gosplan extended control over the whole of Russian industry by replacing the semi-capitalist NEP with a centrally planned economy. In agriculture, collectivisation passed control of farming to the state. Social policy also extended control by ensuring that people's family and sex lives were lived in accordance with the values of the government. In 1936, contraception, homosexuality and abortion were outlawed. Also, divorce was made much more expensive. For example, the cost of a first divorce was 50 roubles, equivalent to one week's wages. Evidently, economic and social policy extended the government's control by ensuring that at work and at home people followed the plan.

In conclusion, the Cult of Personality was a key support for Stalin's totalitarian regime because, along with Socialist Realism, it inspired the people to support the regime wholeheartedly. Nonetheless, the Terror, social policy and economic policy were more important in the sense that they extended Stalin's control. Therefore, overall, the Cult of Personality was only one aspect of Stalin's totalitarian regime.

The conclusion evaluates the significance of the Cult of Personality by developing the argument that it only supported one aspect of totalitarianism. Its overall judgement links back to the definition set up in the introduction and weighs the relative importance of all of the factors mentioned in the essay.

**30/30**

This essay begins with a definition of totalitarianism that shows that the candidate has understood the term. Having defined totalitarianism in terms of total commitment and total control, it examines the way in which a series of factors support these two characteristics. Every paragraph evaluates the extent to which a factor supports totalitarianism, and the continual reference to the definition of totalitarian allows the essay to enter Level 5. There is a lot of detail, and a wide range of factors is discussed, and therefore it gets full marks.

## Key terms

One of the reasons that this essay is so successful is that it begins with a clear definition of the term in the question. Another example of an essay question involving a key term is below. Draw up a plan for your answer to this question. Include a definition of the key term in your introduction and refer back to this definition in subsequent paragraphs.

**How accurate is it to describe Stalin's social policy as a 'Great Retreat'?**

# Section 4:
# The making of a superpower – the impact of the Second World War

## The coming of the war

### The Nazi–Soviet Pact 1939

From 1936, leaders across Europe knew that a major war was likely to break out. Consequently, Stalin tried to make **pacts** with a number of European nations. Germany was eager to sign a **non-aggression deal** with Russia, and therefore, in 1939, the Nazi–Soviet Pact was signed in Moscow.

The Pact committed Russia and Germany to peaceful relations. In addition, it allowed **Hitler** to expand his territory in Eastern Europe, and Stalin to expand his territory in the **Baltic states**. In spite of the Pact, Stalin was under no illusions that there would be war between Russia and Germany. Nonetheless, the Pact bought Russia time to prepare for war.

### The Great Patriotic War: key events

In defiance of the terms of the Pact, Germany invaded Russia in June 1941. By May 1945, Russia had emerged victorious.

| Date | Key event | Details |
|---|---|---|
| June 1941 | Operation Barbarossa | • Germany launched a rapid attack against Russia.<br>• The attack targeted Moscow. |
| September 1941 | Operation Typhoon | • German troops reached the outskirts of Moscow and **Leningrad**.<br>• German attempts to take the cities were repelled by General Zhukov, leader of the Red Army.<br>• German troops laid siege to the cities. |
| August 1942–February 1943 | Battle of Stalingrad | • A protracted battle for the city of Stalingrad, a large industrial city in southern Russia.<br>• Over 1.9 million people killed.<br>• Russian troops succeeded in repelling the German attack. |
| September 1942 | Operation Uranus | • Massive Russian counter-attack.<br>• By the end of 1943, the Russians forced the Germans out of their territory. |
| January 1944 | Ten Great Victories | • Russia captured significant territory in Eastern Europe. |
| April 1945 | Battle for Berlin | • Russian troops reached Berlin.<br>• In May, Russia conquered Berlin, ending the war. |

### How far was Russia prepared for war?

**The Red Army**

Between 1936 and 1938, the **Red Army** had been purged, removing all of its most senior officers. This significantly weakened the strength of the army.

**The Russian economy**

The chaos of the Third Five-Year Plan made economic preparation difficult. Nevertheless, between 1938 and 1941, after the Great Terror, Russian spending on rearmament rose from 27.5 billion roubles to 70.9 billion roubles.

**Spying**

Russia had the best spy network in the world. As a result, Russian spies sent accurate reports to Moscow, detailing the strength of the German army and exact time and date of the planned German attack. However, Stalin did not trust these reports and therefore valuable information was ignored.

## Mind Map

Use information on the opposite and previous pages to add detail to the mind map below.

- the Great Terror
- Stalin's paranoia
- Economic problems

Why was Stalin unprepared for war?

## Support or challenge?

Below is a sample exam-style question that asks how far you agree with a specific statement. Below this are a series of general statements that are relevant to the question. Using your own knowledge and the information on the opposite page, decide whether these statements support or challenge the statement in the question and tick the appropriate box.

'Stalin was responsible for Russia's lack of preparation for war with Germany.' How accurate is this statement?

|  | SUPPORT | CHALLENGE |
|---|---|---|
| Industrial managers lied about production figures. |  |  |
| Stalin negotiated the Nazi–Soviet Pact. |  |  |
| The Red Army was purged. |  |  |
| **Gosplan** was disorganised. |  |  |
| The reports from spies were ignored. |  |  |
| Hitler broke the terms of the Nazi–Soviet Pact. |  |  |
| The Second and Third Five-Year Plans focused on rearmament. |  |  |
| The Cult of Personality had boosted Stalin's popularity. |  |  |

## The cost of the war

## The human cost

### Deaths

Approximately 10 per cent of the Russian population, or 20 million people, died as a direct result of the war. In addition, another 10 million died of injuries or due to their treatment in German prisoner-of-war camps.

### Dislocation

Approximately 85 million Russians ended up living in German-occupied territory during the war. Many of these fled German occupation. Others – approximately 20 million – took advantage of the chaos towards the end of the war to flee communism.

### Women

Women were responsible for the **home front** during the war. In addition to looking after the home and making do on meagre rations, women worked in industry and agriculture. This involved working twelve or eighteen hour days at a factory, and then, during harvest time, working night shifts on a farm to bring in the crops. Additionally, as farm animals and machinery were requisitioned for the war effort, women were yoked to ploughs. Days off were cancelled and the first holiday in four years occurred on 9 May 1945.

## The economic cost

### Total cost

Gosplan estimated that the destruction caused by the Second World War wiped out almost all of the progress made during the first two Five-Year Plans.

### Infrastructure

Russian infrastructure had to be radically reorganised at the beginning of the war. Russian factories in areas at threat from invasion were either destroyed, or dismantled and reassembled to the east of Moscow. At the end of the war, the Germans adopted a **scorched earth policy**, which led to the destruction of even more factories as they retreated. Overall, it is estimated that 32,000 factories and 65,000 kilometres of railway were destroyed during the war.

### Production

The reorganisation of Russian infrastructure, coupled with the **conscription** of many of Russia's most experienced workers, led to a decline in economic production. Russian industrial output in 1942 was only 59 per cent of that in 1940. Grain production was also affected, and in 1942, the Russian economy only produced 36 per cent of the 1940 harvest.

### Rationing

Russian citizens lived on paltry rations throughout the war. The government requisitioned 90 per cent of the grain produced to feed the army. In factory canteens, workers were fed on nettle soup. In the besieged cities of Moscow, Leningrad and Stalingrad, citizens lived on 'blockade bread', made of sawdust. They also ate birds, rats, their pets, their shoes and dead bodies.

##  Simple essay style

Below is a sample exam-style question. Use your own knowledge and the information on the opposite page to produce a plan for this question. Choose four general points, and provide three pieces of specific information to support each point. Once you have planned your essay, write the introduction and conclusion for the essay. The introduction should list the points to be discussed in the essay. The conclusion should summarise the key points and justify which point was the most important.

'The main consequence of victory over Germany in the Second World War was economic devastation.' How far do you agree with this view?

##  You're the examiner

Below are a sample exam-style question and a paragraph written in answer to this question. Read the paragraph and the mark scheme provided on page 3. Decide which level you would award the paragraph. Write the level below, along with a justification for your choice.

'The main consequence of victory over Germany in the Second World War was economic devastation.' How far do you agree with this view?

Economic devastation was certainly a consequence of Russia's victory in the Second World War. Gosplan estimated that the Second World War set the Russian economy back about ten years. This was certainly true in terms of infrastructure. The Germans operated a scorched earth policy as they retreated to stop factories falling into the hands of their enemy. Equally, much of Russia's prime grain-producing land fell into the hands of the Germans early in the war. This meant that for the bulk of the war, Russian harvests remained below their 1940 levels. Harvests were also hampered by the fact that they were brought in by women who had already worked a full day in factories. Therefore, economic devastation was the main consequence of Russia's victory.

Level:    Reason for choosing this level:

_____

_____

## Reasons for victory: Russia at war

### The war economy

Gosplan was ideally suited to organising the war economy. Indeed, it oversaw the relocation of 1,523 factories in the first month of the war. By 1942, economic planners were able to devote 56 per cent of Russia's national income to the war. This was a much higher figure than any of the other countries involved in the war. Moreover, Gosplan ensured armament production doubled between 1941 and 1944.

### The home front

Stalin shrewdly altered the presentation of communist ideology during the war. Propaganda stressed the importance of **patriotism** and it also stopped attacking the Church. Communists believed that religion was a deception designed to fool the **working class** and therefore, ever since the revolution, they had worked to undermine the Church. Stalin ceased attacks on the Church in order to ensure that it backed the government and the war. Patriotism also inspired many to fight due to love of their country. Appealing to the nation and to the Church was more effective at motivating the people than appeals to communism.

### Patriotism

Stalin was under no illusions – communism was unpopular in Russia due to the Great Terror and the failures of Stalin's economic policy. Nonetheless, the Russians were a very patriotic people and Stalin used this to gain support for the war. The war itself was named 'The Great Patriotic War' and Russian soldiers were encouraged to use nationalist nicknames, such as Fritz and Kraut, to refer to the Germans. Patriotism helped Stalin to win the war because it provided the Russians with a reason to fight.

### The Church

Traditionally, communists stood against organised religion. However, the outbreak of war forced Stalin to make an alliance with the Church. Metropolitan Sergei, the leader of the Russian Orthodox Church, proclaimed that Stalin was 'God's chosen leader' and that the fight against Germany was a holy war. In return, Stalin officially closed the communist publication *The Godless* in 1941, and allowed 414 churches to reopen in the final year of the war. The Church, and its promise of heaven, proved to be a great comfort to soldiers who faced death on a daily basis. Religion aided the Russian war effort because it gave soldiers the conviction that God would bless them and their families, even in the event of their death.

### The enemy within

At the beginning of the war, the **NKVD** drew up lists of non-Russian people living in the **USSR** who might be sympathetic to Germany. The NKVD then either relocated these people or murdered them to prevent them aiding the Germans. For example, the Kalmyks, an ethnic group numbering about 130,000, were deported to Siberia following the German invasion. By 1953, following years of brutal treatment, around 60 per cent of those deported had died.

## Delete as applicable

Below are a sample exam-style question and a paragraph written in answer to this question. Read the paragraph and decide which of the options (in bold) is most appropriate. Delete the least appropriate options and complete the paragraph by justifying your selection.

**How far do you agree that the Russian war economy was the main reason for Russian victory in the Second World War?**

The Russian war economy was the **main reason/an important reason/the least important reason** for Russia's victory in the Second World War. For example, Gosplan, Russia's central economic planning agency, devoted 56 per cent of Russia's GDP to expenditure on the war from 1942. This ensured a doubling of arms production between 1941 and 1944. This was a remarkable achievement in light of the fact that for much of this time, Russia's industrial heartland was in the hands of the Germans. At a local level, too, Russian women worked incredibly hard, sometimes working twelve hours at a factory and then through the night bringing in the harvest. In this way, Russia's war economy was the **main reason/an important reason/the least important reason** for Russia's victory in the Second World War because

_____

_____

## Develop the detail

Below are a sample exam-style question and a paragraph written in answer to this question. The paragraph contains a limited amount of detail. Annotate the paragraph to add additional detail to the answer.

**Why did Russia win the Second World War?**

One reason why Russia won the Second World War was the mobilisation of the home front. For example, Stalin understood that traditional communist propaganda would not mobilise the Russian people. Therefore, he appealed to Russian patriotism. He also appealed to the Church in order to help win the war. Stalin knew that the teachings of the Church would inspire soldiers and their families back home to continue the fight for victory. In this way, the home front was crucial to Russia's victory in the Second World War because the careful use of propaganda and the appeal to the Church motivated the Russian people to fight and win.

## Reasons for victory: military campaigns and Allied support

Revised

In addition to the Russian war effort, German mistakes during the military campaigns and the help of Russia's allies were crucial in ensuring Russian victory.

## Military campaigns

Hitler made a series of major tactical errors, which benefited Russia.

- Hitler launched his war against Russia in the east while he still had troops guarding the western front. This divided the German forces.
- He chose to lay siege to Moscow rather than taking the city by force. This allowed the Russian army time to regroup and fight back.
- In June 1942, Hitler sent more troops to fight in Russia. Rather than capturing Moscow and knocking Russia out of the war, he sent the troops to Stalingrad. Here, German forces became embroiled in another siege.

## Allied support

Russia was part of the Grand Alliance, which united Britain, America and the USSR against Hitler. The Grand Alliance was helpful militarily and economically.

### The Grand Alliance

The Grand Alliance helped Russia militarily in the following ways.

- In 1942, Britain and America launched Operation Torch, opening up a front in North Africa. This divided German forces between the eastern front and the new southern front in Africa.
- In 1944, Britain and America reopened the western front, which had been dormant since the **Dunkirk evacuation** of 1940. This further divided German forces, taking pressure off the eastern front.

### Lend-lease

The American scheme **lend-lease** allowed its allies access to American war goods at a fraction of their real cost. This economic aid helped the Russian war effort in the following ways.

- Lend-lease provided 12 per cent of the aeroplanes and 10 per cent of the tanks used by the Russian army during the war.
- It provided 95 per cent of the trains and 66 per cent of the jeeps used by the Russian army to cross Europe.
- It also provided food for the Red Army: approximately 17 per cent of the calorie intake consumed by Russian soldiers came from America.

In total, Gosplan estimated that lend-lease accounted for a mere 4 per cent of the goods used by the Russian army during the war. However, this figure alone underestimates the importance of the scheme. Crucially, the Russian economy was unable to produce food and sophisticated transport goods in large numbers. Lend-lease was of enormous strategic importance because it compensated for the deficiencies of the Russian economy and in so doing aided Russia's victory.

## Identify an argument

Below are a series of definitions, a sample exam-style question and two sample conclusions. One of the conclusions achieves a high level because it contains an argument. The other achieves a lower level because it contains only description and assertion. Identify which is which. The mark scheme on page 3 will help you.

- **Description:** a detailed account.
- **Assertion:** a statement of fact or an opinion that is not supported by a reason.
- **Reason:** a statement that explains or justifies something.
- **Argument:** an assertion justified with a reason.

**How far do you agree that Allied support was the main reason for Russian victory in the Second World War?**

Allied support was an important aspect of the Russian victory but it was not the main reason. Clearly, the lend-lease programme provided essential support in terms of food and transport. In addition, the opening of new fronts in North Africa and Western Europe forced the Germans to overstretch their troops. Nonetheless, the main reason for Russia's victory in the Second World War was Hitler's strategic mistakes. Hitler could have taken Moscow by storm and in so doing knocked Russia out of the war. However, he chose to besiege the city and therefore gave General Zhukov time to organise a counter-attack, and Gosplan time to develop a war economy. Overall, Hitler's mistakes saved Russia from defeat and ensured her victory.

In conclusion, Allied support was the main reason for Russia's victory in the Second World War. The lend-lease programme was very important because Russia's war economy had important weaknesses. Collectivisation meant that Russia was not very good at making food. Similarly, the Five-Year Plans were good at producing raw materials in large quantities, rather than sophisticated machines. Lend-lease filled both of these holes. The Allied military also helped by opening up fronts in North Africa and Western Europe. German military mistakes contributed too. Hitler divided his forces in Russia between three cities and therefore failed to take any of them. This is why Russia won the Second World War.

## RAG – Rate the timeline

Below are a sample exam-style question and a timeline. Read the question, study the timeline and, using three coloured pens, put a red, amber or green star next to the events to show:

- red – events and policies that have no relevance to the question
- amber – events and policies that have some significance to the question
- green – events and policies that are directly relevant to the question.

1. **How far did Stalin's economic policy aid Russian victory in the Second World War?**

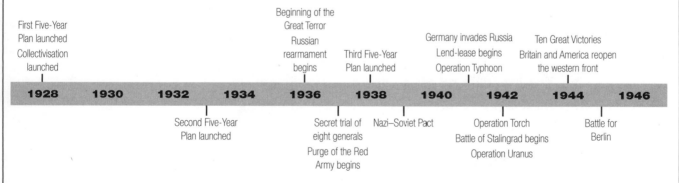

Now repeat the activity with the following questions. You could use different colours, or number your stars 1, 2 and 3.

2. **How far was Stalin's economic policy the main reasons for Russia's victory in the Second World War?**

3. **How far was Stalin responsible for Russia's victory in the Second World War?**

## Superpower

The end of the Second World War led to a major realignment in world politics. First, the empires that had dominated the world for more than a century gave way to two new superpowers: Russia and America. Secondly, the Grand Alliance fell apart, leading to a **Cold War** between the two superpowers and their allies.

Russia's emergence as a superpower was based on its geographical influence, its economy and its military might.

### Geographical influence

By 1946, Russia had gained a **sphere of influence** in Eastern Europe, which acted as a **buffer zone** against its capitalist enemies in the west. This helped Russia to become a superpower because it allowed Russia to effectively control half of Europe.

- Russia established communist regimes across Eastern Europe in countries such as East Germany, Czechoslovakia, Hungary, Poland and Bulgaria.
- These **satellite states** were not fully independent and Russia controlled their economy and foreign policy.
- Russia entered into an informal military alliance with its satellite states, suggesting that these countries would fight alongside Russia in any future conflict.

### Economy

At the end of the Second World War, Stalin launched the Fourth Five-Year Plan, which aimed to restore Russia's economic might. This assured Russia's superpower status by allowing Russia to compete with America in terms of military spending.

- The Fourth Five-Year Plan made Russia the fastest growing economy in the world.
- By 1952, total industrial production was twice that of 1940.
- The focus of the Fourth and Fifth Five-Year Plans was heavy industry and rearmament, ensuring that Russia was prepared for any future war.

### Military might

Russia's superpower status was also based on the fact that it had one of the strongest militaries in the world.

- In 1946, Russia had an army of 3 million men, the largest army in the world.
- The Fourth Five-Year Plan devoted 7.4 billion roubles to defence spending, almost 2 billion roubles more than defence spending in the run-up to the Second World War.
- In 1949, Russia developed its own atomic bomb, catching up with the Americans.
- In 1953, Russia developed its own hydrogen bomb, again rivalling America's military might.
- Immediately after the war, Russia began developing rockets to be used as missiles against America. These would later be used in Russia's conquest of space.

---

### Russia at the time of Stalin's death

Stalin died in 1953. During Stalin's time in power, Russia was transformed from a backward agricultural economy into an industrial superpower. However, this came at the cost of millions of lives due to dekulakisation, the Great Terror and the Second World War.

---

## Mind Map

Use the information in Section 4 to add detail to the mind map below.

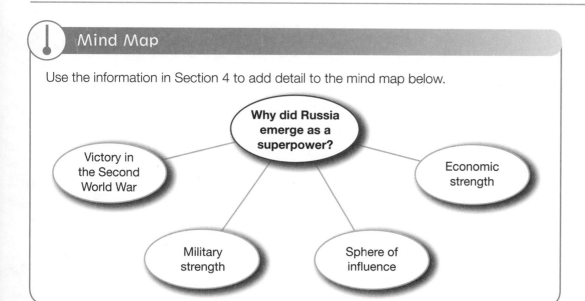

## Complex essay style

Below are a sample exam-style question, a list of key points to be made in the essay, and a simple introduction and conclusion for the essay. Read the question, the key points, and the introduction and conclusion. Rewrite the introduction and the conclusion in order to develop an argument.

**Why did Russia emerge as a superpower after the Second World War?**

### Key points

- Victory in the Second World War
- Military strength
- Sphere of influence
- Economic strength

### Introduction

There were four main reasons why Russia emerged as a superpower after the Second World War. These were its victory in the Second World War, its military strength, its sphere of influence in Eastern Europe and its economic strength.

### Conclusion

In conclusion, there were four key reasons why Russia emerged as a superpower after the Second World War. The most important reason was its victory in the Second World War. This played a more significant role than all of the other factors.

## Recommended reading

Below is a list of suggested further reading on this topic.
- Richard Overy, *Russia's War* (pages 99–124). Penguin, 2010.
- Dmitri Volkogonov, *Stalin: Triumph and Tragedy* (pages 452–463). Crown, 1991.

## Exam focus

Below is a sample A-grade essay. Read the essay and the examiner's comments around it.

**Why did Russia emerge as a superpower following the Second World War?**

The introduction lists three factors that will be discussed in the essay, but it could be improved if it introduced an overall argument.

> Russia became a superpower following the Second World War for three main reasons. First, victory in the Second World War gave Russia a sphere of influence in Eastern Europe. Secondly, Russia's economy became the fastest growing in the world. Finally, at the end of the Second World War, Russia had the largest army in the world and soon developed a nuclear bomb.

This paragraph begins with a clear focus on the question.

> One reason why Russia became a superpower was its sphere of influence. The Red Army marched across Eastern Europe in 1944. Following the war, Russia turned this territory into a series of satellite states. These states were not fully independent because Russia was able to effectively control their economic and foreign policy. Additionally, these new satellite states, which included Czechoslovakia, Hungary, Poland and East Germany, formed a buffer zone that prevented an immediate military assault on Russia

The paragraph ends by explaining why Russia's geographical position helped it emerge as a superpower.

> herself. Russia's geographical influence in Eastern Europe was a key factor in Russia's emergence as a superpower because it created a series of friendly states that would join with Russia in any future military conflict and work with Russia to ensure Russia's continued greatness.

This paragraph makes effective use of information regarding the period 1928–41, and shows its relevance to the post-war period.

> The Russian economy was another key reason for the emergence of Russia as a superpower following the Second World War. The first three Five-Year Plans, which took place between 1928 and 1941, laid the foundation for Russia's post-war economic growth. Stalin's emphasis on heavy industry led to the growth of industries that were well suited to the production of war goods. Additionally, industrial work trained a generation of workers who, following the war, could develop Russian industry further. Certainly, the Second World War had done much to destroy the achievements of the early Plans. For example, around 32,000 factories and 65,000 kilometres of railway were destroyed as part of Germany's scorched earth policy. Nonetheless, following the Second World War, Russia became the fastest growing economy in the world. Russia was helped by the satellite states, which traded exclusively with Russia. Clearly, the Russian economy was a key reason for Russia's emergence as a superpower because it was well suited to military preparation and it was built on a strong foundation for growth.

Russia's military might is the final reason for her emergence as a superpower following the Second World War. Russia's growing economy allowed Soviet planners to devote 7.4 billion roubles to defence spending during the Fourth Five-Year Plan, which ran from 1946 to 1950. This was even more (2 billion more) than Russia had spent in the run up to the Second World War. On top of this, the Russian army kept 3 million men in uniform following its victory in Europe. This was the largest army in the world. Russia's military might was even more impressive because of the buffer zone that Russia had won in Eastern Europe following the end of the Second World War. America, Russia's Cold War enemy, would have to cross the whole of Eastern Europe and face the largest army in the world, meaning that Russia was impregnable. Finally, Russia's military might was increased in 1949 following the successful development of its atomic bomb. Developing an atomic bomb was an extremely expensive business and only possible because of Russia's growing economy. In 1953, Russia went yet further, developing a hydrogen bomb and powerful rockets which allowed Russian missiles to target America. Once again, these were very expensive projects, which were only possible because of Russia's growing post-war economy. In this way, Russia's superpower status was guaranteed by its military strength and its ability to create and deploy the dreaded nuclear bomb.

In conclusion, Russia became a superpower following the Second World War because its sphere of influence gave it an important military advantage and brought it wealth through trade. Its economy provided the funds necessary to rearm and develop expensive nuclear and missile technology, and its military, including its new atomic bombs, rivalled those of the west.

This paragraph applies extremely detailed economic data.

The candidate effectively links this factor to another factor discussed in the essay, by relating Russia's military might to Russia's geographical position.

Precise dates are used very effectively in this paragraph.

The conclusion shows the way that the three factors linked together to make Russia a superpower.

26/30

This essay gets a mark low in Level 5. It gets this mark because the three factors discussed are linked together and in this sense, the essay demonstrates sustained analysis. In addition, the supporting examples are focused and detailed. However, it cannot go beyond low Level 5 because the introduction and conclusion do not reach an overall judgement.

## What makes a good answer?

You have now considered four sample A-grade essays (see pages 16, 32, 46 and above). Use these essays to make a bullet-pointed list of the characteristics of an A-grade essay. Use this list when planning and writing your own practice exam essays.

# Glossary

**Baltic states** Three countries with coastlines on the Baltic Sea: Estonia, Latvia and Lithuania.

**Black market** The illegal trading of goods and services.

**Bolshevik Party, The** Former name of the Russian Communist Party.

**Bolsheviks** Members of the **Bolshevik Party**.

**Bourgeois** The term used by Karl Marx to describe the middle class.

**Buffer zone** A geographical area that divides two hostile states.

**Capitalism** An economic system based on free trade and the private ownership of property.

**Central Committee** A group of about 120 senior communists who were responsible for managing the Communist Party between **Party Congresses**.

**Cold War** A conflict between the United States and Russia, starting after the Second World War and ending in the late twentieth century. Although it is described as a 'war', the conflict was mainly ideological and there was never any formal fighting between the two countries.

**Collective farm** A farm that brought together between 100 and 150 families. Collective farms were controlled by the government. They replaced small-scale farms that were run and controlled by one or two families.

**Collectivisation** The process of merging several small farms in private ownership to create large farms under state ownership.

**Communist** A person or state that is identified with communism. Communists believe that history moves through a series of stages and that **capitalism** should be replaced by an economic system in which goods are distributed more equally. The final stage of history is known as communism. It is characterised by the distribution of goods according to need and the absence of government, money and a free market.

**Conscription** Compulsory enrolment in the army.

**Consumer goods** Products that are designed to be used by individuals for their own benefit, such as shoes, refrigerators or cigarettes.

**Cult of Personality** Attempts in the Russian media to idealise Stalin and Lenin. The Cult encouraged ordinary Russian citizens to treat Lenin and Stalin as heroes and geniuses.

**Doctrine** A set of beliefs.

**Dunkirk evacuation** The evacuation of British troops from northern France in the summer of 1940.

**Factionalism** The organisation of a group within the party that opposes the party's leadership. Factionalism was considered a crime by communists following Lenin's ban on factions in 1921.

**Factions** Groups of people within a political party who share a common set of beliefs and who are in opposition to the leadership of the party. Lenin banned factions in 1921.

**Free market** An economic system in which people are able to trade without interference from the government.

**GDP** Gross Domestic Product: the total wealth produced by a country in a given period.

**General Secretary** The most important administrative post in the Communist Party. Stalin held this position from 1922 until his death in 1953.

**Gosplan** The organisation responsible for economic planning in Stalin's Russia.

**Grain Procurement Crisis** A period in which Russian peasants were reluctant to sell grain and other agricultural products to the government, leading to food shortages.

**Gulags** Prison **labour camps**.

**Hitler** The leader of Germany from 1933 to 1945.

**Home front** The civilian contribution to the war effort.

**Kirov Group** A group of high-ranking Russian politicians who supported Kirov. They argued for the moderation of Stalin's policies, in particular for a greater emphasis on the production of **consumer goods** during the second Five-Year Plan.

**Komsomol, The** Communist youth organisation.

**Kulaks** Rich peasants.

**Labour camps** Prison camps built in the late 1920s to house tens of thousands of prisoners. The prisoners were forced to work on big construction projects such as dams or factories. Prison camps were often built in extremely cold parts of Russia. Prisoners were fed barely enough food to survive. As a result, prisoners were effectively worked to death.

**Labour productivity** A measure of the amount produced by workers in a specified period.

**Left wing** During the 1920s, this section of the Communist Party argued against compromises with **capitalism** and in favour of policies it believed to be fully **socialist**.

**Lend-lease** A scheme set up by the American government, which allowed America's allies to buy military equipment, weapons and food on long-term credit during the Second World War.

**Leningrad** Russia's second city. It was known as Petrograd until 1924, when it was renamed Leningrad to commemorate Lenin's death. Since 1991 it has been known as St Petersburg.

**Lenin's *Testament*** A document written in 1922 in which Lenin set out his thoughts on leading members of the Communist Party.

**Machine tractor stations** Government-owned tractor depots from which tractors could be rented by **collective farms**.

**Magnitogorsk** A major industrial city created to produce steel during the First Five-Year Plan.

**Marxist** A follower of the teachings of Karl Marx, a nineteenth-century German philosopher and revolutionary. His most famous works include *The Communist Manifesto*, which set out a theory of history and revolution, and *Capital*, which explained and criticised the workings of **capitalism**.

**Nationalism** The belief that all nations should govern themselves without interference from other nations. It often goes hand in hand with national pride: the feeling that there is something special and admirable about a person's own country.

**New Economic Policy (NEP)** A semi-capitalist economic policy introduced by Lenin in 1921 to help revive Russia's economy after a famine.

**New industries** Industries that were more sophisticated than heavy industry. These included the chemical and electrical industries.

**NKVD** The Russian secret police.

**Non-aggression deal** An agreement to maintain peaceful relations between two or more countries.

**October Revolution** The revolution in which the **Bolshevik Party** seized power in Russia.

**Pacts** Formal deals between countries.

**Party Congress** A meeting of over 1,000 senior communists representing the whole of Russia, with responsibility for major policy decisions.

**Patriotism** Love of your country.

**Patronage** A form of power that is based on the ability to promote the career of another.

**Peasant** A person who works on a farm.

**Personal rule** Government that is based on an individual, rather than a party or group of individuals.

**Petrograd** See **Leningrad**.

**Politburo** The most senior committee in the Communist Party.

***Pravda*** The newspaper of the Russian Communist Party.

**Purges** The process whereby people were removed from the Communist Party for corruption and political crimes.

**Rabkrin** The Workers' and Peasants' Inspectorate: a body set up by Lenin to investigate allegations of corruption in the Communist Party. It had the power to discipline and sack members of the Communist Party.

**Red Army** The Russian Army.

**Red specialists** Members of the working class who were educated and given positions of responsibility within Russian industry.

**Requisitioning** Formally demanding the use of somebody else's property or produce.

**Right wing** During the 1920s, this section of the Communist Party believed that it was too soon to pursue fully **socialist** policies. Therefore, it favoured policies that compromised with **capitalism**.

**Russian Civil War** A conflict between the communist government and all those that opposed it, which ran from 1918 to 1921.

**Satellite states** A state that is formally independent, but under heavy influence from another state.

**Scorched earth policy** The decision to destroy crops, factories and property during a retreat rather than let them fall into enemy hands.

**Show trials** Trials that are designed as propaganda. They do not establish the innocence or guilt of the defendants, but aim to publically humiliate enemies of the government.

**Socialism** An ideology and a political system based on the belief that people should be treated equally. Communists believe that this occurs after **capitalism** but before full communism.

**Socialist** The word socialist can be applied to a person, policy or society. A socialist person is someone who believes in **socialism**. A socialist policy is a policy that is likely to make society more equal. A socialist society is a society that is run according to socialist principles. In theory, this would mean a society where people are treated equally.

**Socialist Realism** The artistic form favoured in Russia under Stalin. It had two main characteristics. First, it focused on the activities of workers and peasants working under Stalin's leadership to build socialism on **collective farms** and in Russian industry. Secondly, the paintings and sculptures were 'realistic' in the sense that they looked like photographs.

**Soviet** A shortened form of the term 'Soviet Union', usually referring to things related to or coming from the Soviet Union. It can also be used to refer to Russia.

**Speculators** People who make money by buying and selling on the **black market**.

**Sphere of influence** A geographical area in which one country dominates.

**Stakhanovite movement** A movement designed to increase **labour productivity**. Workers were rewarded for extraordinary efforts and achievements. The first Stakhanovite was the miner Alexei Stakhanov.

**Theorist** A thinker: someone who is concerned with ideas and who comes up with theories.

**Totalitarian** A form of modern dictatorship in which the regime attempts to control all areas of life. A totalitarian regime expects total commitment, co-operation and enthusiasm from its citizens.

**USSR** Union of Soviet Socialist Republics. Established in 1922, the USSR was a federation of states, including the Ukraine, Georgia and Russia. In theory, these states were independent, but in practice they were dominated by Russia. All of the states in the Union were run by the Communist Party.

**Working class** People who work in factories.

*Yezhovshchina* A popular term that meant that the methods of Yezhov and the **NKVD** had taken over all aspects of Russian life.

# Timeline

| | |
|---|---|
| **1924** | Lenin's death |
| | Thirteenth Party Congress: the Triumvirate defeat the Left Opposition |
| **1925** | Zinoviev and Kamenev move to the left wing of the Communist Party |
| **1927** | Fifteenth Party Congress: the Duumvirate defeat the United Opposition |
| **1928** | Emergency economic measures introduced: Stalin abandons the NEP |
| | First Five-Year Plan launched |
| **1929** | Twenty-Five Thousanders sent out |
| | Dekulakisation begins |
| | Compulsory collectivisation introduced |
| **1930** | Stalin halts collectivisation |
| **1931** | Collectivisation restarts |
| **1932–34** | Famine |
| **1933** | Second Five-Year Plan launched |
| **1934** | Seventeenth Party Congress: Congress of Victors |
| | Kirov murdered |
| **1935** | New school curriculum introduced |
| **1936** | Homosexuality, adultery, contraception and abortion banned |
| | Wedding rings reintroduced |
| | Trial of the Sixteen |
| | Yezhov becomes leader of the NKVD |
| **1937** | Trial of the Seventeen |
| | Doctrine of sharpening class struggle |
| | Secret trial of Red Army generals |
| **1938** | Third Five-Year Plan launched |
| | Trial of the Twenty-One |
| | Yezhov arrested |
| **1939** | Nazi–Soviet Pact |
| **1940** | Trotsky assassinated |
| **1941** | Germany invades Russia |
| | Collectivisation completed: all farms in Russia are collectivised |
| | Communist publication *The Godless* is closed down |
| **1945** | Russia conquers Berlin; end of the Second World War |
| **1949** | Russia develops an atomic bomb |
| **1953** | Russia develops a hydrogen bomb |
| | Stalin dies |

# Answers

## Section 1: The struggle for power 1924–29

### Page 5, Complete the paragraph: suggested answer

Personal factors were very important in Stalin's emergence as leader of Russia. For example, **most members of the Soviet government thought that Stalin had no obvious failings. They described him as 'the grey blur', suggesting that there was nothing controversial or outstanding about him. In contrast, the other contenders for power had clear flaws. Trotsky was highly intelligent and a brilliant speaker. However his talents meant that many in the Communist Party viewed him as arrogant. Bukharin was popular within the Party, but some older communists thought that he was too young to lead the Party. Zinoviev and Kamenev were seen as too cautious because they had criticised the October Revolution and Zinoviev had avoided the fighting during the Civil War.** In this way, personal factors played an important role in Stalin's emergence as leader because Trotsky's arrogance, Bukharin's youth, and Zinoviev and Kamenev's cowardice made these contenders unpopular with the Communist Party. However, Stalin had no obvious flaws.

### Page 5, Identify an argument

Paragraph 1 contains the argument.

### Page 7, Spot the mistake

The paragraph does not get into Level 4 because although it contains a lot of relevant detail, it does not use this to explicitly answer the question. In this sense it is not an analytical response.

### Page 9, Eliminate irrelevance

One reason why Stalin emerged as leader of Russia was the debate about the economy within the Communist Party. The Party was divided between the left wing, who favoured rapid industrialisation, and the right wing, which wanted to continue with the NEP. The NEP favoured the peasants as it allowed them to trade freely and make a profit. ~~Stalin was born into a peasant family in Georgia.~~ The right wing argued that this was necessary as peasants formed the majority of the population and their loyalty was important for the survival of the government. The left wing criticised the NEP because it wasn't fully communist. ~~Communism was an idea developed by Karl Marx, a famous German philosopher in the nineteenth century. He thought that history went through different economic stages.~~ The left wing argued that rapid industrialisation was necessary if communism was to survive. The economic debate was very important to Stalin's emergence as leader of Russia because he was able to use the debate first against the left wing, and then, once the NEP started to fail, against the right wing. In this way, he knocked out his opponents.

### Page 9, Develop the detail: suggested answer

Economic debates played a major role in Stalin's emergence as leader of Russia. The Party was divided over this issue. Some communists **such as Bukharin on the right wing of the Party** wanted to continue with the NEP as they felt this would make the Communist Party more popular in Russia. **The NEP was extremely popular with the peasants as it imposed only low taxes and allowed them to trade freely.** Others **such as Trotsky on the left wing of the Party** wanted rapid industrialisation for ideological reasons. **They believed that the dictatorship of industry was a fully communist policy.** In the late 1920s, the NEP began to fail badly **– between 1926 and 1927, grain production in Russia fell by 5 million tonnes –** and this had an impact on the debate. For example, Stalin switched sides **from the right wing to the left wing** in order to win more support. Previously, **in 1925**, Zinoviev and Kamenev had also switched sides, but this had not benefited them **as they abandoned the NEP at a time when it was very popular. Bukharin remained committed to the NEP and consequently lost support.** In this way, economic debates decreased support for all contenders for power, except Stalin. Only Stalin used the debates to his advantage.

### Page 11, Turning assertion into argument: suggested answer

The debate over Trotsky's idea of permanent revolution was crucial to the outcome of the leadership struggle because **it allowed his enemies to persuade the Party that his ideas would lead to a war with capitalist nations that Russian people did not want, thus discrediting him within the Party.**

Stalin's arguments for Socialism in One Country played an important role in helping him become leader of Russia because **they appealed to the nationalism of the majority in the Party.**

The debate over economic policy was more important in deciding the outcome of the leadership struggle than the debate over foreign policy because **Stalin used economic policy first to defeat the left and then to defeat the right, whereas he could only use foreign policy to discredit his opponents on the left.**

## Page 13, You're the examiner

The paragraph should be awarded Level 4 as it shows clear focus on the question and provides accurate, relevant and detailed supporting evidence.

## Section 2: Transforming the Soviet Union – collectivisation and industrialisation

## Page 19, Complete the paragraph: suggested answer

One reason why Stalin launched his 'revolution from above' in 1928 was that the NEP had failed. By 1928, the NEP had allowed steel production to recover to 1913 levels, that is to say 4 million tonnes were produced. However, iron production under the NEP was still considerably less than it had been before the First World War: iron production in 1913 had been 4.2 million tonnes, whereas in 1928 it was only 3.3 million tonnes. What is more, grain production under the NEP fell in 1927 and only partially recovered in 1928. **Clearly, the failure of the NEP played an important role in Stalin's decision to launch the 'revolution from above' because it meant that a radical change in policy was necessary to ensure continued economic growth.**

## Page 21, Spot the mistake

The paragraph does not get into Level 4 because it describes the process of collectivisation rather than focusing on the question.

## Page 23, Turning assertion into argument: suggested answer

The First Five-Year Plan was highly successful in terms of production because **it led to a massive increase in the amount of raw materials produced.**

The First Five-Year Plan was more successful in terms of quantity of materials than quality of materials because **although production rose, much of what was produced could not be used as it was of extremely low quality.**

The First Five-Year Plan did not benefit the people of Russia as much as the NEP because **the production of raw materials, such as steel and coal, did not lead to an increase in living standards, whereas the NEP focused much more on consumer goods.**

## Page 25, Identify an argument

Paragraph 2 contains the argument.

## Page 25, Develop the detail: suggested answer

Stalin's economic policy was most successful during the Second Five-Year Plan. For example, transport improved. **The Moscow Metro opened in 1935 and the Volga Canal was completed in 1937.** In addition, consumer goods became more widely available to Russian workers. **Between 1933 and 1937, the production of consumer goods doubled.** Labour productivity also increased **with the introduction of the Stakhanovite movement**. There was even greater success in terms of heavy industry, **with coal production doubling,** and by the end of the Plan, rearmament was happening too. **For example, government spending on rearmament rose by 13 per cent between 1933 and 1937.** But there were problems. Housing and hygiene were a disaster **as many new houses lacked running water and 650,000 people in Moscow had no access to a bathhouse**. Diet and clothing remained poor for many workers. **For example, a queue of 6,000 people formed outside a shoe shop in Leningrad in 1934.** There were also new inequalities **with 55,000 senior communists enjoying benefits such as holiday homes and limousines**. In this way, the Second Five-Year Plan was much more successful than the First, but it was not a complete success because although productivity improved, the living conditions of many workers remained poor.

## Page 29, Eliminate irrelevance

Stalinism did lead to greater sexual equality in the world of work. In the period 1928–41, the number of women employed in industry rose from 3 million to over 13 million. ~~This could be because of the Five-Year Plans, which aimed to transform Russia from an agricultural economy to an industrial one.~~ What is more, the number of women employed on collective farms also increased and a number of women, such as Pasha Angelina and Maria Demchanko, became national celebrities as successful members of the Stakhanovite movement. Even so, women were still not fully equal. ~~On farms, conditions were dreadful because of dekulakisation and the Great Famine.~~ Also, even in 1940, women only accounted for 41 per cent of workers in industry and on average they earned around 40 per cent less than men. In this way, greater sexual equality was achieved in the workplace, but full sexual equality was not achieved because wage differences suggest women's work was not valued as highly as that of men.

## Section 3: Persecution and control – the totalitarian regime

### Page 35, Spot the mistake
The paragraph does not get into Level 4 because it does not provide detailed supporting evidence.

### Page 37, Complete the paragraph: suggested answer
**One of Stalin's aims for the Great Terror was to eliminate his former rivals.** For example, the Trial of the Sixteen in 1936 eliminated Zinoviev and Kamenev and their key supporters from the Moscow and Leningrad Parties. The second trial – The Trial of the Seventeen – in 1937, targeted those who had supported Trotsky during the 1920s. Trotsky himself was tried and found guilty at this trial, even though he was not present. The final trial was against Bukharin and those who had supported the right wing in the last phase of the leadership struggle, including Yagoda who had initially backed Bukharin after the Duumvirate split. In this way, the Great Terror clearly eliminated Stalin's former rivals because the three Moscow show trials resulted in the conviction of the leading figures who had opposed Stalin in the 1920s.

### Page 37, Eliminate irrelevance
One of Stalin's aims for the Great Terror was to gain greater control of the Red Army. The Red Army was a powerful and disciplined fighting force that could have been used to overthrow Stalin. Stalin was paranoid and, in the case of the Red Army, there was good reason for his paranoia. The Red Army was established and run for many years by his archrival Trotsky, ~~who would be assassinated in Mexico in 1940~~. Evidence of Stalin's concern about the army is found in the secret trial of eight generals in 1937. ~~This was not the first time Stalin had turned against Trotsky's allies, as he had turned against Zinoviev and Kamenev in 1927 after the Fifteenth Party Congress.~~ Having found the generals guilty of treason, Stalin purged a further 34,000 soldiers from the army. Clearly, one of Stalin's aims for the Great Terror was to gain better control of the army because he could not count on its support for his leadership.

### Page 39, Identify an argument
Paragraph 2 contains the argument.

### Page 39, Turning assertion into argument: suggested answer
Terror escalated massively under Yezhov because **he introduced the 'conveyor belt system' which allowed the NKVD to work more effectively than before.**

Outside Moscow, factory managers, rather than Communist Party members, can be considered the main victims of the Great Terror because **Stakhanovites used the opportunity to turn against their managers as they considered their managers, rather than the Party, to be the greatest obstacle to the success of the Five-Year Plans.**

### Page 41, You're the examiner
The paragraph should be awarded Level 3 as it is accurate, but tells the story of the show trials rather than specifically focusing on the question.

### Page 43, Develop the detail: suggested answer
Art was a significant form of social control in Russia in the 1930s. Stalin introduced a new form of art called Socialist Realism. **Socialist Realist art was realistic and reflected socialist values.** There were Socialist Realist Paintings showing happy workers and peasants. **For example 'Voting to Expel the Kulak from the Collective Farm' by S. Y. Adlivankin shows peasants enjoying their role in dekulakisation. There was also** Socialist Realist literature celebrating the successes of Stalin's policies. **For example, the novel 'Forward, Oh Time' by Valentine Kataev describes the excitement of working at a steel factory during the Second Five-Year Plan. Finally,** Socialist Realist architecture created grand places for workers. **For example, the Teatralnaya Metro station was designed to look like a palace and yet be accessible to workers.** All of these forms of art acted as a form of social control because they promoted communist values and inspired workers to support the regime.

## Section 4: The making of a superpower – the impact of the Second World War

### Page 51, You're the examiner

The paragraph should be awarded Level 4 as it shows clear focus on the question and provides accurate, relevant and detailed supporting evidence. Nonetheless, the analytical link at the end of the question is assertive rather than explanatory and therefore it does not get to the top of the level.

### Page 53, Develop the detail: suggested answer

One reason why Russia won the Second World War was the mobilisation of the home front. For example, Stalin understood that traditional communist propaganda would not mobilise the Russian people. Therefore, he appealed to Russian patriotism. **For example, he called the war 'The Great Patriotic War' and encouraged Russian soldiers to use nationalist nicknames such as Fritz and Kraut to describe the Germans.** He also appealed to the Church in order to help win the war. **Communists believed that religion was deceptive, and since the revolution Russian communists had attacked the Church. However, Stalin ended the attacks on the Church, ceasing the publication of 'The Godless' and allowing 414 churches to reopen. In addition, he made an alliance with Metropolitan Sergei, the leader of the Church. Metropolitan Sergei then described Stalin as 'God's chosen leader'.** Stalin knew that the teachings of the Church would inspire soldiers and their families back home to continue the fight for victory **as the promise of heaven would be a comfort in the face of suffering and death.** In this way, the home front was crucial to Russia's victory in the Second World War because the careful use of propaganda and the appeal to the Church motivated the Russian people to fight and win.

### Page 55, Identify an argument

Paragraph 1 contains the argument.

# Notes

# Notes

# Notes